T0274714

REBIRTH
OF THE BLUES

The Rise of Chelsea Football Club
in the Mid-1980s

Neil Fitzsimon

First published by Pitch Publishing, 2023

Pitch Publishing
9 Donnington Park,
85 Birdham Road,
Chichester,
West Sussex,
PO20 7AJ
www.pitchpublishing.co.uk
info@pitchpublishing.co.uk

ISBN 978 1 80150 396 9

Typesetting and origination by Pitch Publishing
Printed and bound in Great Britain by TJ Books, Padstow

CONTENTS

Introduction 7

Chapter 1 11

Chapter 2 28

Chapter 3 40

Chapter 4 56

Chapter 5 72

Chapter 6 82

Chapter 7 90

Chapter 8 108

Chapter 9 119

Chapter 10 130

Chapter 11 138

Chapter 12 146

Chapter 13 155

Chapter 14 162

Chapter 15 178

Chapter 16 193

Chapter 17 208

Chapter 18 222

Chapter 19 233

Chapter 20 239

Epilogue 251

INTRODUCTION

WITH APOLOGIES to Daphne du Maurier and her classic novel, *Rebecca*, I feel the need to paraphrase her classic opening line to that masterpiece:

'Last night, I dreamt I saw Chelsea win away.'

Strangely, it's always the same game; the Blues' visit to Selhurst Park to face Crystal Palace on 20 November 1971. In the dream I can still recall the biting cold that afternoon as Gallagher, my wingman, and I, had one of my gloves each as he had neglected to take into account just how cold it was on the terraces that day. On a grey afternoon that saw Chelsea come away with a somewhat unconvincing 3-2 win, the two memories that consistently feature in my dream include Ossie's brilliant third goal for the Blues when he swivelled with his back to the goal in one graceful, fluid movement to turn and fire in an unstoppable shot high into the Palace net beyond keeper John Jackson's despairing dive. This fine effort put the Blues 3-1 ahead in what seemed an unassailable lead. Unfortunately the second part is the calamitous mix-up in the Blues' defence that led to Gerry Queen pulling a goal back for the home side and putting Palace right back in the game. Fortunately, Chelsea withstood a late onslaught to take the points that day.

Another memory as clear today as it was all those years ago is that just before Palace scored their second goal, the Chelsea away support started singing, 'We'll be running round Wembley with the cup.' Seeing that we'd just reached the semi-final of the League Cup where we were drawn to face Spurs, this all seemed to make perfect sense to the Blues' massive following at Selhurst Park that day. The only trouble was that mid-chant, the Chelsea fans' thunderous celebrations were silenced when Palace scored their second goal, which was handed to them on a plate. It was precisely at that moment that our own war of words erupted with some old bloke standing behind us. He was the stereotypical flat-capped moaner who watched the game with a world-weary cynicism. His attitude clearly defined that old football saying of 'it was better in my day, when men were men, not these long-haired ponces that play the game today'. He then snidely remarked, 'You'll be running round Wembley with fuck all with a defence like that.'

Even though Gallagher and I were furious with the old boy, we decided to ignore him, the reason being that like the thousands of Chelsea fans there that day we were too choked that we'd handed Palace an unlikely lifeline back into the game. The last thing on our mind was to be concerned with some miserable old git who was shouting his mouth off. There were still ten minutes left for Chelsea to hang on as Palace threw everything at us but the kitchen sink. Me and Gallagher were no strangers to cursing and swearing our way through games. This was the law of the terraces back then when foul language was the accepted norm. However, the moaning old windbag behind us proceeded to tap us on the shoulder and inform us that he'd never heard such disgusting language from two young lads, and that we should be ashamed of ourselves, whereupon Gallagher snapped back, 'Who do you support, then?'

'Palace,' the old duffer replied.

'Fuck me!' Gallagher spat back. 'You talk about us being ashamed? What about the shit team you support?'

The old boy looked apoplectic with fury. It's something of a mystery, and God only knows why he did it, that he was standing there that day surrounded by the massed ranks of Chelsea supporters. Surely the old boy would have been happier among the other Palace fans. But no, this was most probably the place that he'd watched his team play for years and years, so nothing was going to budge him. Still, it has to be said that this elderly gentleman had the last laugh when the following March, his prediction bore fruit after Chelsea had somehow managed to lose the League Cup Final 2-1 to Stoke City after dominating most of the game. The old boy's bitchy remark of 'you'll be running round Wembley with fuck all' had now become a cold, hard fact. I've often wondered if that crotchety old geezer remembered me and Gallagher that blustery afternoon in March 1972 as Chelsea failed in their third cup final in as many years. If he did, I should imagine he took some sense of pleasure that indeed, he'd very much had the last laugh after all.

It's strange that that Palace game has been a recurring dream over the years, considering all the matches I went to in those days – it hardly stands out as one of the Blues' most memorable displays. But there you are. The one thing that none of us has any control of is the subconscious and its many vagaries.

1

ANOTHER TIME in the Blues' history I recall vividly is the summer of 1977. This should have been a period to look back on with fondness, seeing that Chelsea had regained their place in the First Division after being promoted from the Second Division, finishing as runners-up to Wolves. But the sickening blow of manager Eddie McCreadie's departure had left a bitter taste in the mouths of everyone connected with the club. His exciting young side looked to be on the verge of great things when out of nowhere, the man who'd masterminded Chelsea's resurgence had vanished into the ether. What made the situation even more depressing was that he was replaced by the anonymous Ken Shellito, a reserve team coach. While Shellito was a fine full-back for the Blues whose career was cut short by an injury, it was hardly an appointment that stirred the blood around Stamford Bridge. It almost seemed perverse that Chelsea had let go of a man who could have been one of their greatest managers over a petty argument about buying Eddie Mac a new car, to replace the club's old minibus that he'd been using since he took over in April 1975. The whole situation beggared belief. In my opinion, and that of many others, the heart had been ripped out of our club when Eddie Mac left the Bridge that day in July 1977 to head for the USA. A talent like that doesn't come around too often, if at all, and the most sickening aspect of the whole sorry affair was that the club itself had been the architect of its own downfall.

I wasn't exactly filled with much confidence when new boss Shellito announced that he'd be adapting our playing style for a return to the top flight. A much more tactical approach would be introduced rather than Eddie Mac's high-energy style of play which seemed to me to be a ludicrous decision. After all, that approach had got us promoted. Why change it now? But Shellito was the boss and it seemed he was determined to make his own mark and dispense with Eddie Mac's way. Those comments by Shellito put the fear of God into me, and I suspect many other Chelsea fans. Adapting to a new way of playing seemed to say to me that Shellito was scared of the higher-class opposition that we would be facing in the coming season.

Look, I don't want to be hard on poor old Ken; after all, the task that he had taken on from Eddie Mac was hardly an enviable one as the club was still in dire financial circumstances and there would be very little money for new signings, if any, that summer. Basically, the players who had got us promoted would now be asked to steer Chelsea through in what would undoubtedly be a long, tough, hard season. The disparity between the three sides promoted that year from the Second Division was highlighted when Nottingham Forest splashed out a record fee for a goalkeeper when they signed England regular Peter Shilton to bolster their ranks. It was an inspired acquisition by Brian Clough as that year Forest went on to triumph by claiming the First Division championship and they also added the League Cup for good measure by beating Liverpool 1-0 in a replayed final at Old Trafford.

The summer of 1977 has gone down in the national consciousness as the summer of punk. It was also the summer that marked the Queen's Silver Jubilee. The street parties and celebrations were played out to the accompaniment of Johnny Rotten and the rest of the Sex Pistols, much to the horror of the Auntie BBC, who, in their infinite wisdom, decided that the nation should not be subjected to the prospect of the Pistols' 'God Save the Queen' single occupying the number one position in the charts that week of the Jubilee celebrations. So, in an act of what was the prime example of the Nanny State, the BBC proceeded to ban it from its shows and stations, thereby denying the Pistols their rightful place at the top of the charts. Instead we had to endure the very pedantic cover of 'The First Cut Is the Deepest' by the faux-Scottish crooner Rod Stewart. I would advise anyone who has heard Stewart's rather lame attempt at covering what is in my estimation a great song to check out the original cover version of the Cat Stevens tune, by a certain P.P. Arnold. In a word, it knocked poor old Rod's version into oblivion as far as I'm concerned.

The summer of 1977 was my first full summer with my new girlfriend Vicky. I'd like to say that it was all plain sailing. I'd like to, but that would be a lie. Like many blokes of my age, the actual reality of having a steady girlfriend was a lot more difficult than I had bargained for. It was, indeed, my initiation into the moods and whims of the female mind. These were lessons I had to learn pretty quickly. I soon realised that the concept of having a girlfriend was not as straightforward in reality.

Chelsea were due to play West Bromwich Albion away at The Hawthorns on the opening Saturday of the football season, 20 August 1977, which coincided with my first holiday with a girlfriend in tow. Where were we bound for? Somewhere exotic, you might think. A destination that conjured up dreams of crystal-blue seas and golden beaches that stretched into the distance. Well, not quite. I decided that my new Spanish girlfriend should follow me in my childhood footsteps, and consequently we found ourselves travelling to Ramsgate for a week in a B&B. Still, I was keeping my promise that if she stuck with me I would show her a good time. The trouble was, as she rather bitterly said after that week's holiday, it always seemed to be other people having the good time, which I thought was a bit harsh.

I had loved Ramsgate when I was a kid. It was the holiday destination for thousands of Londoners, especially those south of the river, as the Kent coastline was only a relatively short distance away from the Smoke. In reality, Ramsgate was nothing less than a home from home for Londoners. There were pie and mash shops in abundance with jellied eels and seafood stalls peppered along the seafront. When I was going to Ramsgate in the 1960s, the town was in its pomp. The beaches were crowded, there were no vacancies in the B&Bs and hotels, and queues outside cafes – not to put too fine a point on it, the place was alive and thriving. There was a strange pecking order among Londoners in those days. Those of us who went to Ramsgate looked down on people going to nearby Margate as being somewhat common. Meanwhile, the genteel holidaymakers who took their yearly break in Broadstairs (once the home of Charles Dickens, no less) looked upon the people who visited Ramsgate and Margate as nothing short of the epitome of the unwashed oiks from the lower-class areas of the capital.

Sad to say that by 1977, Ramsgate had seen better days. As I showed Vicky around the seafront and esplanade, it was obvious that my boyhood holiday home was in a very sad state of decline. The big amusement arcade looked tatty and run down, belying its rather grand name of 'Merry

England' complete with a Britannia edifice on its roof. That Morrissey track, 'Every Day is Like Sunday', sums up the sorry state of affairs of what was once a proud Kent coastal town had descended into, highlighted in the lyric, 'It's just a seaside town that should've closed down.' Still, as the saying goes, we had to make the best of it. Unfortunately our B&B didn't help matters. It was, in a word, appalling. The food was disgusting and the endemic decrepitude of Ramsgate in general seemed to have seeped insidiously through the walls of this ghastly dump.

Still, at least I could look forward to the Blues' debut back in the top flight that Saturday afternoon. I told Vicky that I would be listening to the radio back in our room, leaving her in no doubt that if she had any ideas about going to the beach, she should quickly dismiss those thoughts from her mind. After all, I told her, we have to get our priorities right, and I'm sorry but Chelsea come first. Unsurprisingly that comment did not go down very well at all.

The Blues' trip to West Brom wasn't the commentary game on the radio so I'd have to wait nervously for updates to see how we were faring in our baptism of fire. Anxiously, I laid on that decrepit old bed in our shabby bedroom, hoping against hope that Chelsea would somehow manage to beat the Baggies. To be honest, I would have taken a point, anything to get us off to a decent start. At half-time it was still goalless. So far, so good. That was until the 68th minute when West Brom took the lead from the penalty spot. Disappointingly, Chelsea then proceeded to cave in and conceded two further goals to complete a thoroughly miserable afternoon, as the home side ran out comfortable 3-0 winners. According to the match reports, Chelsea had held their own for long parts of the game until the deadlock was broken with that spot kick, and had then gone on to fall apart as the gulf in class and experience between the two sides became glaringly obvious.

To say I was disappointed would be an understatement. In fact I was in a foul mood and slumped into a childish sulk. Vicky tried to placate me but that only made things worse as she didn't have a bloody clue about football. How could she share my pain? I didn't need words of consolation. I just needed her to shut her trap and leave me alone. Thankfully, my conscience eventually got the better of me. After all, this was the first day of our holiday and it would have been totally unfair of me to ruin it for her due to my ever-changing moods through my fanaticism regarding the Blues' fortunes.

'Let's go out,' I said. 'To a pub that has a restaurant in Pegwell Bay, where I used to go when I was a kid.'

'Sounds nice,' she replied.

True, it did sound nice, but instead of having a nice meal and a civilised drink, I proceeded to get totally smashed on numerous pints of Stella Artois.

The last memory I have of that evening is of trying to watch *The Prisoner*, the brilliant Patrick McGoohan series from the 1960s which we'd both been obsessed with. Unfortunately, owing to the fact that I'd consumed so much beer, I fell asleep in the TV room at the B&B, whereupon Vicky had to somehow help me stagger up the stairs to our seedy little bedroom. My next memory of that bacchanalian night was waking up the following morning with the mother of all hangovers, and to my shame I found myself firmly in the doghouse.

Chelsea's next game would be against Birmingham City in midweek at the Bridge. In those days it was a lot more difficult to find out the result of an evening fixture, especially when you were on holiday. After my poor display on the Saturday night and my reaction to the debacle at

West Brom, I could hardly say to Vicky that I needed to get back to the B&B early that evening so that I could find out how the Blues had got on. These were the days when the quickest way to find out the result if you didn't have access to a radio was to watch the late news on either the BBC or ITV. There, the scores would be announced by somebody like the newsreader Reginald Bosanquet, who quite obviously couldn't have given a toss about the game, as he delivered the scores in a half-mocking, weary voice that was a personification of his contempt for all the plebs hanging on his every word. As soon as the phrase, 'Here are tonight's football results,' was uttered, I could swear that my heart always used to miss a beat. So, having to play the dutiful boyfriend, I had to face the fact that my agony would not be relieved that day.

The following morning, after breakfast, I rushed down to the newspaper stand on the seafront to nervously scan the paper for that all-important result. Gleefully, I read that Chelsea had beaten the Brummies 2-0 thanks to goals from Gary Stanley and Ray Lewington. The only blight on that game, which was played in a torrential rainstorm, was the fact that Steve Finnieston – aka Jock – had missed a penalty. Still, all said and done, it was a vital win and our first points of the season. The crowd of just over 18,000 was disappointing for our first home game back in the top flight, but as previously mentioned, the game was played during a deluge so perhaps the low attendance was not through a lack of interest from the Stamford Bridge faithful, but most probably down to the appalling weather.

Being obsessed with what kits Chelsea were wearing, I noticed from the photos in the newspaper that the Blues were now in a slightly altered strip from the previous season's. Being a traditionalist, I was not in favour of the Umbro logo that was now adorning the shoulders and sleeves of the shirt. Gone also was the traditional white stripe on the blue shorts, replaced with another type of stripe that consisted of that bloody Umbro logo again. Personally, I much preferred the plainer kit we'd worn for the previous two seasons.

This was an era when kit manufacturers were starting to leave their mark on club colours, and, to this day, I loathe some of the monstrosities that the Blues have been lumbered with over the years. In my view I think Nike have been culpable for some of the worst examples we've ever seen the Blues wear in recent times. Apart from the kit we wore in the 2021 Champions League Final victory over Manchester City, I've not been exactly enamoured with some of their feeble efforts. I honestly believe that some of their designers at Nike must either be colour blind or have no knowledge of the Blues' traditions. The Adidas kit of the Premier League-winning season of 2016/17 was great and makes me wonder why we ever signed up with Nike in the first place – money, I should imagine. It's notable that when Chelsea and Nike got together to produce a retro version of our 1970 FA Cup-winning shirt, it outsold all of their other efforts instantly. As the saying goes, sometimes less is more. That beautiful, iconic kit still stands alone as the pinnacle of any strip that Chelsea have ever worn.

* * *

After our victory against Birmingham, our next game was at the Bridge again on the Saturday Vicky and I were due to leave Ramsgate. Just my luck, I thought, that I'd missed our first two home matches back in the First Division. Still, my hopes were high that we'd see off Coventry City to record our second successive home win. I wasn't exactly sorry to see the back of that bed and breakfast. For one thing, the meals had been so disgustingly bad that I tried out a little experiment. Suspicious that the same piece of toast had been left on our breakfast table every day without change, I left some teeth marks in one of the crusts. My suspicions were confirmed when I discovered that the same bit of toast had indeed been on our table for three consecutive days.

They also had a rule that you weren't allowed back in your room until four in the afternoon, a constant practice in those days among the harridans that passed for landladies. It really was a bloody cheek. I can recall countless times when I was a kid, walking around with my family, patiently waiting for the time when we would be allowed back in our rooms. On sunny days that wasn't a problem as we spent all day on the beach. However, on rainy days, we found ourselves traipsing around the seafront and high street of Ramsgate, trying to find something to do before we went back to the comfort of our dingy digs – digs that we'd actually paid for. Unbelievable! Thankfully, this is now a thing of the past, yet it still shows what a tolerant lot we Brits are. I can think of no other country where such a rule would have been accepted, let alone obeyed.

As if the meals weren't bad enough, there was also the strange case of the person who was occupying the room adjacent to ours. On a daily basis we could hear strange noises and mumbling coming from that godforsaken cell. We subsequently found out that it was the son of the proprietor, who seemed to spend all of his time in this dreary tomb. Heaven knows what was wrong with him. It was, all in all, very strange indeed. I fully expected Mr Rochester from *Jane Eyre* to furnish us with an explanation. But sadly this was not to be.

Our coach was due to leave Ramsgate bus station at 5pm, and, yet again, I was desperate to find out how the Blues had done against Coventry. As we boarded the coach,

I seized my chance. I asked the driver if he knew anything about the day's footie results.

'I'll put the radio on for you, mate,' he replied.

Nervously, I stood there alongside the driver while the other passengers had to push past me to take up their seats on the coach. Then I heard Chelsea's result come in. We had lost 2-1. I was totally gutted. Our second defeat in three games, and we'd lost our unbeaten home record that we'd held since Orient had beaten us at the Bridge back in the spring of 1976. I was beginning to wonder if the promised land that we'd all craved for might in the end turn out to be nothing short of a disaster. When you've enjoyed a season like 1976/77, where our defeats had been few and far between, this was all a bit of a wake-up call. While we had looked far too good for the Second Division, it now seemed apparent that we might not be good enough for the demands and rigours of the top flight. I was very subdued on the journey back to Hertfordshire. That empty, sick feeling that I always endure every time the Blues are beaten was back – and with a vengeance. Still, I thought, I'd better not risk another massive outburst, as it seemed to me that Vicky was gradually getting quite tired of my ridiculous behaviour every time Chelsea came up short. I decided just to keep my mouth shut and hope against hope that this foul mood would eventually pass.

However, there was one bright spot that raised my spirits no end on that tedious journey home. When we stopped for a refreshment break at some awful halfway house that had obviously done some sort of deal with the various coach companies, we were all duly expected to exit the coach, whereupon we would march like lemmings to the grotty pub with some sort of snack bar where we could purchase watered-down beer and sandwiches that had seen better days – all at an inflated price.

'We'll sit this one out,' I said to Vicky. 'Is that OK?'

'Fine,' she said. 'Look at the queue for the toilets.'

It was then that I noticed on the coach directly opposite us, a kid of about nine or ten years old was pulling faces at us. First of all we both ignored him, but after a while I was starting to get fed up with this little buffoon. I can quite clearly recall he had the type of face that needed a good slap. His head was shaped like a butterball with a pudding basin haircut that fully convinced me that this little sod would one day turn into an even bigger Herbert. Finally, I could stand no more of his baiting and in double quick time I gave him the two-finger salute followed by the single finger and that most offensive of gestures signalling what I was convinced he would one day turn into – a wanker!

Then, the cheeky little sod repeated everything I'd just done and gave it back to us in spades. He seemed to find this hysterical as he jumped up and down on his coach seat. So pleased was he, by his demonstration of how quickly he could learn those signs, that he then made the schoolboy error of taking it one step too far and decided to give me one final two-finger salute before our two coaches went their separate ways. It was at that precise moment that his mum, who was sitting alongside this kid's dad in the seat in front, noticed what her errant son was up to. Horrified at what she'd seen, she then proceeded to give the little bugger a right backhander that put a stop to his little game in an instant. While he was rubbing his recently cuffed head, his mum made him apologise to us. I could see that the little kid was protesting that she'd got it all wrong, and that we were just as guilty as him. Sadly for him, she didn't believe a word of it and gave him another cuff round the head for good measure. The last we saw of this little monster was his pudding face with tears streaming down his fat rosy cheeks, resorting finally in him perpetrating the most childish of all gestures which was to poke his tongue out at us. And then he was gone.

I've often wondered how he turned out and if he remembers that bizarre incident in that car park all those years ago. Did we feel guilty about the punishment he received from his mama? No, not one bit. In fact we laughed our heads off. How cruel, you might think. But in those days, seeing mums and dads belting their kids was not at all unusual. Today, that kid would most probably report his parents for child abuse but back then, no one on that coach took any notice of a mother chastising her child in public. Having said that, this type of thing never happened from either of my parents. Though to be honest I most probably deserved it many times.

* * *

School, however, was another matter. Unlike today, we lived in fear of certain teachers and they thought nothing of dishing out corporal punishment. The more lenient of this particular breed would give you a slap across the back of the legs, but some sadists who passed for educators preferred the ruler across the hand, or the slipper. The biggest psycho I ever came across was the headmaster at my junior school who gleefully used to dish out his favourite form of punishment with a bat that had a smiley face on one side, which was shown to his victim before the beating, and a crying face which was shown to the poor boy or girl – yes, girls as well – after they'd received their thrashing by this complete and utter nutcase.

The worst example, however, occurred when I was in the second year at senior school. We had a maths teacher, Mr Bailey, who also took us for games. Bailey, with his chiselled face and swept-back blond hair, resembled something that Adolf Hitler would have held up as the prime example of Teutonic manhood. Like the Nazis, Bailey was a complete bastard. Before one games lesson, my mate Tony asked Bailey if he could be excused from taking part in the game of football we were due to play as he had a bad stomach ache and had been sick a couple of times. 'Nonsense!' Bailey replied to Tony's plea. 'If you can't run around, you can go in goal.'

Tony, like all schoolkids in those days, dutifully complied. During the game, which Bailey was refereeing, Tony looked ashen-faced. It was obvious to all of us kids that he wasn't at all well. Still, Bailey totally ignored his pleas to be excused and berated Tony, 'Get on with it, boy!'

It was then that Tony threw up in the goalmouth and fell to the ground clutching his stomach. What followed next still leaves me in a state of disbelief to this day. Bailey actually stood over Tony, prodding him with his foot, shouting, 'Get up, boy!'

Thankfully, one of the other kids playing in that travesty of a game had the gumption to go and get another teacher, who took one look at Tony and told someone to phone for an ambulance which thankfully arrived within minutes. And thank God it did. Because it most probably saved Tony's life seeing that his so-called feigned illness turned out after all to be a burst appendix. You might think that, all things considered, Mr Bailey was for the high jump. But these were different times and not one word was ever said about his brutish behaviour. In those days teachers were held in a mixture of high regard and fear by both pupils and parents, and the whole episode was swept under the carpet.

There was some form of rough justice coming Mr Bailey's way when a gang of fifth-formers decided to give him a taste of his own medicine on their last day at school before venturing out into the world of work. I was one of the second-years told politely to fuck off as me and my classmates tried to get into the boys' changing room for our games lesson. Those fifth-formers scared the living daylights out of us puny little second-years, so not one of us protested too much and we quickly scarpered and ran for cover. I don't know for sure what happened behind the closed doors of that changing room, but when we saw Bailey later in the afternoon he was sporting a black eye. I'd like to think that in some small way, Bailey had finally got what he so richly deserved. As the old saying goes, what goes around comes around.

After this brief history of corporal punishment in the educational system of the 1960s, I hope you can begin to understand why that incident in the coach with the little brat being belted by his mother hardly caused anyone who witnessed it to bat an eyelid.

* * *

On the Sunday morning after the 2-1 home defeat to Coventry, the papers didn't exactly make happy reading for all Blues fans. Apparently Chelsea had been outplayed by Coventry, who had effortlessly moved into a two-goal lead by half-time. According to reports, Coventry had spurned numerous chances to increase their lead. Their profligacy almost came back to haunt them when Tommy Langley pulled a goal back for the Blues, but what I found to be most alarming was that, according to the papers, Coventry had been a class above the home team. Who would have thought that the once-mighty Chelsea were now considered second best to a team like Coventry?

When I first started going to Chelsea in 1968, I and many others saw the likes Coventry as nothing more than makeweight outfits that consistently flirted with relegation. But now, to my horror, apparently, they were considered to be a superior side to the Blues. Still, it was no good harking back to the past. In August 1977 it was apparent that Chelsea would have a fight on their hands to preserve their place at football's top table. Two more defeats followed in quick succession, both against Liverpool at Anfield. The first was a League Cup tie that the home side won comfortably 2-0; the second loss, a few days later in the league, pretty much followed the pattern of the first match as Liverpool ran out 2-0 winners for the second time in a week. In both games Liverpool's new signing, Kenny Dalglish, had been a thorn in Chelsea's side. The Scot already looked to be an upgrade on the recently departed former Kop hero Kevin Keegan. Just when a lot of people thought that Liverpool would sadly miss the all-action dynamic style of Keegan, it seemed regretfully that for everyone apart from the Liverpool faithful that in Dalglish they had found an even better player, which made the £440,000 that Liverpool had paid for him that summer nothing short of a bargain. Though those two results were disappointing, you could hardly call them unexpected. This was an era when Liverpool dominated the English game and as far as Chelsea were concerned, our focus was on the teams around us and below us, not on such teams as Liverpool who occupied the lofty heights of the First Division.

The first match I went to that season was against Derby County at the Bridge. The game itself was pretty undistinguished apart from one incident. Derby's Leighton James had tormented the Blues' defence all afternoon. The former Burnley winger always seemed to play well against Chelsea and this day was no exception; the Welshman was having one of those days when everything seemed to come off for him. That was until Bill Garner, who'd hardly featured at all in the promotion-winning season of 1976/77, suddenly found himself back in favour under the new boss

Ken Shellito. Garner was a rather gangly, awkward type of centre-forward whose main strength was in the air. But believe me, he was no Ossie or Hutch. That being said, he hardly came across as a player with a vindictive side to his game, but it seemed that day that poor old Bill had had quite enough of James's flicks and tricks and proceeded to totally clean him out with a savage tackle that resulted in James being stretchered off. It was nothing less than GBH. The Derby players went mad trying to get Garner sent off but, in those days, you could get away with tackles like that and still stay on the field. After the game, the Derby boss Colin Murphy blasted Shellito, piously claiming, 'Any manager who condones such tackling must surely look to his conscience.' He might as well have saved his breath as no punishment was handed out to Garner, who walked away from that incident totally scot-free.

What about the result, you might enquire. Well, after Gerry Daly had put Derby ahead from the penalty spot, the game descended into what can only be described as nondescript. Once again, Tommy Langley came to the Blues' rescue when he equalised in the second half and that's the way it finished. Still, at least it was a point. But a 1-1 draw against a mediocre Derby side was hardly expected to set the pulses racing.

On top of all that, the following Saturday we were due to face Manchester United at Old Trafford. To say I wasn't very hopeful would be an understatement. With only one win so far, it was a bit of a stretch of the imagination that we'd actually come away from Manchester that sunny afternoon in September with anything. But yet again Chelsea, as they so often do, upset the odds by running out 1-0 winners after Garner's second-minute goal stunned the home crowd. Could this be a harbinger of an upturn in the Blues' fortunes? Well, not really. As autumn turned into winter, a long struggle to remain in the top flight lay ahead of us. It seemed that every decent result was usually followed by a couple of defeats just for good measure. It was almost as though the footballing gods were saying, 'Don't get ahead of yourself.'

2

AT THE beginning of November, we actually achieved back-to-back home wins for the first time in that campaign with a 1-0 success over Bristol City followed by an even more impressive 1-0 victory over Brian Clough's Nottingham Forest, who were riding high in the league that year. In fact, riding high is a bit of an understatement as Forest would go on to claim the title in what was their first season back in the First Division, as well as the League Cup. You might wonder how Forest, who'd finished below us in the promotion campaign of 1976/77, could suddenly appear out of nowhere to win two major trophies, while Chelsea, along with the rest of the top flight, were left in their wake. From Chelsea's point of view, the club was still broke so basically the side that had got us promoted would now have to prove themselves worthy of their place in the top tier with no funds available. Sadly, the Blues most definitely, as the saying goes, did not have a pot to piss in whereas Forest had invested in England keeper Peter Shilton and Scottish internationals Archie Gemmill and Kenny Burns. Not forgetting that they were led by one of the most brilliant partnerships, the managerial team of Brian Clough and Peter Taylor. It soon became startlingly clear just how far Chelsea had fallen behind this brilliant Nottingham Forest side.

Both of the goals in those two successive home wins were scored by a certain Trevor Aylott, who had suddenly broken into the first team. He'd headed the winner against Bristol City, then followed that up a week later when he blasted the ball high into the net past Shilton at the Shed end. Ken Shellito, I'm afraid, got a bit carried away with Aylott's heroics and proceeded to announce that the youngster was a mixture of Ossie and Hutch blended together. It sounded good, I suppose, but sadly it was no more than wishful thinking as Aylott's brief appearance in the spotlight was just that – very brief. After a few more appearances he disappeared back into obscurity, never to be seen in the blue shirt again.

This book is going to concentrate on the two bipolar seasons of 1982/83 and 1983/84, so I will just pick out some of my memories from the years between 1977 and 1982. I would like to say that they were highlights but I'm afraid they might come across as a bit of a lament, as the club's fortunes declined in a most alarming fashion. A few weeks after the Forest victory, the Blues visited Maine Road to face Manchester City, who proceeded to carve us apart as we were buried beneath an avalanche of goals and lost 6-2. City winger Peter Barnes was in unstoppable form that day, and tormented Ray 'Butch' Wilkins's brother Graham to the extent that the Chelsea full-back was eventually given his marching orders after yet another desperate challenge on Barnes.

By the time Christmas came around, the Blues were still dangerously close to the wrong end of the table. True, there were a few heartening results including a fine 3-1 away win over fellow strugglers Wolves, who were finding life back in the top flight just as troublesome as we were. Then there was the vital home victory over West Ham on 27 December 1977, when Hammers goalkeeper Mervyn

Day's calamitous mistake allowed the Blues to take all the points. What made this result even more notable was that the game was played just 24 hours after Chelsea had been on the end of a 3-0 thumping from Arsenal at Highbury, a situation that would never occur in the modern day. Three matches in a week is now regarded as a punishing schedule.

Five days after the West Ham game, Chelsea came away from St Andrew's after beating Birmingham City 5-4 in a nine-goal thriller. The only negative that day was that we'd actually been leading 5-2 with just two minutes left, only to let the home side back in. Those two late goals had both players and fans of Chelsea praying for the final whistle. But there is no doubt about what would go down as the highlight of that baptism of fire back in the old First Division: the two home games against Liverpool.

When the draw was made for the third round of the FA Cup, I was horrified, yet somehow resigned, when I found out that we would face Liverpool at the Bridge. Liverpool at that time were head and shoulders above everybody else in the country as well as Europe. They'd already won the European Cup in 1977 for the first time and would go on to retain it the following May against Club Brugge. So it was in hope, rather than expectation, that I made my way to the Bridge that cold January day in 1978.

But how wrong could I be? Chelsea tore into their vaunted rivals straight from the kick-off and were unfortunate to be only leading by Clive Walker's brilliant effort by half-time. Worse was to follow for the Scousers in the second half as they unbelievably collapsed when the Blues quickly added two more goals, through Steve Finnieston, who'd failed so far to match his free-scoring efforts from the previous season, and a fine effort from Tommy Langley after he latched on to a woeful back-pass to hit an angled drive past the helpless Liverpool keeper,

Ray Clemence. Though Liverpool quickly pulled one back, they still looked decidedly out of sorts, so it came as no surprise when Walker scored his second with an easy finish to put Chelsea 4-1 ahead. In all honesty, I should imagine every Blues fan there that day at the Bridge couldn't believe what they were seeing. The sight of mighty Liverpool being humbled is still one of my most cherished memories to this day. Though Kenny Dalglish scored a consolation goal, it was nothing more than that and the Blues left the pitch to a standing ovation while Liverpool started working out what excuses they could make for their pathetic performance. A remarkable victory was made even more impressive when you consider that our talisman and captain, Wilkins, had missed this epic game through injury.

Another abiding memory I have of that day apart from Walker's two goals was the beautifully considered, sublime midfield performance by the veteran Charlie Cooke. Now well into his 30s, he still was a class act and somehow seemed to glide over the pitch with an arrogance and swagger that recalled the early days of the 1970s. There was another incident in this game that I still find appalling to this day, and the culprit was a certain Emlyn Hughes, who tried, unsuccessfully I might add, to get Bill Garner sent off for allegedly punching the Anfield cry-baby. I've watched that fiasco many times since that day, and it really is appalling – the way Hughes clutched his face while wildly writhing on the ground. Garner just stared at him with disdain, telling him to get up, but no, Hughes just carried on with his ridiculous posturing until the referee told him to get up, in no uncertain terms. It was quite apparent that Garner's so-called punch was nothing more than Hughes's pathetic attempt to get the Chelsea man sent off. In that era of the 1970s this type of play-acting was unheard of in the national game, and the fact that an ex-England skipper had resorted to such execrable behaviour to get a fellow professional player sent off really was the nadir of everything we stood for in football in those days. The credo was that you played hard, but you played fair.

Let's be honest, Hughes has never held a warm place in my heart, or I suspect in any of the hearts of the Chelsea faithful. I know it's not good form to speak ill of those who've passed on, but I've decided to give it a go. Firstly, he was the player who broke Ossie's leg in October 1966 while playing for Blackpool in a League Cup tie at Bloomfield Road. Another black mark against Hughes is that after that dreadful challenge, he didn't contact, let along visit Ossie in hospital, to offer his apologies. No, instead he was rewarded by being transferred to Liverpool shortly afterwards. I've got no doubt that Hughes's tackle cost the Blues the 1967 FA Cup Final against Spurs when we limply went down 2-1 to the hated enemy. You might say that's just conjecture. Well, I would remind you that Ossie's replacement at Wembley that day was Tony Hateley. I rest my case.

Ossie's career, which had seen him becoming one of the most exciting young talents in the game, was almost over before it started. Ossie always said that he never got back that half-yard of pace that he'd had before the injury, and in my opinion it wasn't until the 1969/70 season that we began to see the Osgood we'd witnessed when he broke into Tommy Docherty's brilliant young Chelsea side in the mid-1960s.

After that FA Cup victory over Liverpool, I was looking forward to reading the papers the following day, something that had been all too rare that season. Most of the reports were pretty glowing. However, one grinch still found it necessary to vent his spleen by saying, and I quote, 'If this young Chelsea side thinks that that was the real Liverpool they were playing today, then they should think again.' I bet this journalist had wished that he'd kept his stupid mouth shut because when Liverpool returned to play us in a league game at the beginning of March, yet again, the so-called 'Mighty Reds' were given another hiding at the Bridge. With the match goalless at half-time, our hopes seemed to have been dashed when Phil Neal put Liverpool ahead from the penalty spot. But it seemed that the Blues hadn't read the script when shortly afterwards Tommy Langley scored what was in my estimation, and I've seen quite a few others, his best goal for the club when he equalised with a thumping drive past Ray Clemence to bring the scores level. It really was a great finish as Langley brilliantly brought the ball under control, swivelled, and sent a vicious, hurtling drive into the net. And so a game that Liverpool seemingly had in their pocket now swung away from them as Chelsea cashed in on two more defensive howlers, the first of which was down to none other than our old friend Emlyn Hughes. At the final whistle, Chelsea ran out 3-1 winners. To have beaten Liverpool twice in a few months was undoubtedly the highlight of our season – make no mistake about that.

Yet still the press undercut our joyful celebration stating that this was a Liverpool side in decline, and then added more insult to injury by saying that Chelsea were living in a fool's paradise if they thought that this result actually meant something – which only goes to prove that the Blues have never been the media's favourite club. The backbiting and lack of interest in the Chelsea's recent successes, especially on Sky Sports, is shocking. The coverage of our brilliant second Champions League victory over Manchester City in the 2021 final in Porto was little more than derisive and half-hearted, almost like they were in the midst of an incredible sulk that the favourites, City, the darlings of the English press, had failed to claim the one trophy that they craved above any other prize in the game.

Still, I'm quite comfortable to accept that we are one of the most hated teams in the country. Like many other Chelsea fans, I wear that badge with pride. They can dish up all the invective they like – as long as we keep on winning trophies, who cares?

* * *

Our league form after beating Liverpool was still a cause for concern, and any step forward was quickly followed by two steps back in the opposite direction. A few weeks later I went with my mate Mick to Upton Park to see his team, West Ham, taking on Chelsea which was undoubtedly a vital game in the relegation dogfight as the Hammers, like us, were up to their necks in it. Chelsea, who were playing in an all-yellow strip, took an early lead through Bill Garner's thumping header. My elation was tempered when I thought to myself, how the hell are we going to hang on to this advantage, taking into account that we had a defence that had been leaking goals consistently all season? At half-time we still had the lead, and well into the second half we still looked comfortable with David Hay showing all Chelsea fans what they'd been missing throughout the season when injury, yet again, had reduced his performances to a handful of games. The minutes seemed to drag by like they always do when you're hanging on to a lead.

The classic example was the seven minutes added to the 90 in our Champions League Final victory over Manchester City. Where that time came from, I'll never know. I mean, apart from Kevin De Bruyne's injury, when he came off second best after Antonio Rüdiger's over-zealous challenge. I was screaming at the TV, 'What is the ref playing at!' Those seven minutes were some of the longest of my life. I'm sure that everyone with blue blood coursing through their veins remembers that awful moment in the last seconds when Riyad Mahrez's shot seemed to be looping into the net beyond Edouard Mendy. For anyone concerned with Chelsea, it was a joyous relief when the ball sailed harmlessly wide. That was City's last chance, and seconds later the most glittering prize in club football was ours for the second time.

The reward back in 1978 was not so high. At Upton Park, our ambitions were a little more prosaic: staying in the First Division. This seemed within our reach until Bill Garner went off with an ankle injury to be replaced by young Tommy Langley. Nothing strange in that, you might think – one centre-forward replacing another. Sadly, this was not the case as shortly afterwards there was an ugly clash when West Ham centre-half Tommy Taylor challenged for a loose ball with Chelsea keeper John Phillips. In all fairness to Taylor, the ball was there to be won. Phillips was extremely brave as he tried to gather the ball at the feet of the onrushing Taylor. Disastrously for the Blues, Taylor's boot connected with Phillips's head with a sickening crunch. Was it a fair challenge? Well, let's just say, it was the challenge of a player whose team were losing 1-0 at home in a vital relegation battle and staring at the drop.

It was pretty obvious that this was a serious injury. Phillips lay motionless in the goalmouth and by the looks on the faces of both sides, it became quite apparent that he would take no further part in the afternoon's proceedings. It was then that it dawned on me with sickening clarity that Chelsea, having used our permitted one substitute – yes, that's right, in those days there was only one substitute allowed – would therefore be down to ten men and one of our outfield players would have to go between the sticks. That dubious honour fell upon the shoulders of poor Tommy Langley. As he donned that green jersey you could tangibly feel that the game was now definitely swinging in the home side's favour.

As John Phillips was being carried off on a stretcher by the St John Ambulance men, he passed right by where myself and Mick were standing by the players' tunnel. His face looked a right mess, all battered, bruised and bloody. Most of the crowd around me, mainly West Ham I have to say, gave him a nice round of applause as all rivalry was forgotten for a moment at seeing a player so obviously in a bad way. That is apart from one brainless twat who spewed forth a vile stream of abuse at the stricken stopper. You might think that this torrent of invective was perpetrated by some young lout who knew no better. But you'd be wrong. In fact it was a bloke who must have been in his 60s, and of course, he was in the uniform of the old terrace tosser: the perennial flat cap. It was, in a word, staggering, that this stupid old wreck was still spewing his stream of insults, at his age. I was apoplectic with rage at this old duffer and spun him round by his shoulder and asked him politely, 'What the fuck are you playing at?'

'I pay me money! I can say what I like!'

'You, mate,' I snapped back, 'are nothing but a total fuckwit!' I was just contemplating whether I should give him a slap when Mick pulled me back and told me to calm down. It was a wise move on Mick's part as the Old Bill were already starting to show an interest in the fracas. It was apparent to everyone standing around me just where my allegiances lay which in normal circumstances could have proved to be a bit tricky. But so shocked were the Hammers supporters standing near me at their elderly compatriot's outburst that they just looked on with embarrassment at the whole sorry episode. That injury to Phillips proved to be, as I suspected, the point at which the match now turned in West Ham's favour.

Though we held on for a short while with Langley making a few decent saves, his inexperience was laid bare when Trevor Brooking's corner somehow eluded him and ended up in the back of our net. The Blues were now under terrific pressure as the home side finally woke up to the fact that the points were there for the taking. Chelsea bravely held on as their beleaguered defence withstood one attack after another. It would have been some form of justice if we had come away from Upton Park with something but unfortunately football can be a cruel game at the best of times. And a bad day got a whole lot worse when the home side scored two goals in injury time to take the points with a 3-1 win. It was a horrible, sickening feeling to lose that game. The sense of injustice was overwhelming. My first thought was where was that old bastard now, such was the red mist descending in front of my eyes. I sought out that flat-capped twat with a savage vengeance, but I was foiled in my pursuit as it seemed the silly old fool had decided to move somewhere else on the terraces. Now, looking back, it was just as well. It would have been dreadful when I was asked by my mum, 'How was the football today?'

'Well, we lost, Mum. And by the way, I got involved in a fight with a bloke old enough to be my grandad.'

The silence was awkward between me and Mick on the way back from Upton Park. He was delighted that his team had won but I also think he was quite aware that any words of consolation would be slung back straight into his smug face. The final footnote on this episode – West Ham were relegated that season and Chelsea stayed up.

After a few drinks in the West End that night, I was feeling slightly better – a feeling that I knew would evaporate as soon as I woke up the following morning when the fact that we'd lost to West Ham would hit me like a ton of bricks. One bright spot was that my mum had successfully carried out the task that I'd set her the previous day, and that was to buy tickets for the Elvis Costello gig at the Hemel Hempstead Pavilion. I was at that time, and still am today, obsessed by Costello and couldn't wait to see him live. After thanking Mum for getting the tickets, I was beckoned by my sister to come into the kitchen where she informed me that when Mum went to the box office to buy the tickets, she asked the cashier in her poshest voice, 'Three tickets for the Elvis Costello show, please' – a phrase uttered in that special way that mums have when they haven't a clue what they're talking about. Of course my sister, who had been standing next to Mum at the box office, burst out laughing at Mum's self-conscious request. From then on, it became a standing joke in my family much to my amusement and much to my mum's annoyance.

* * *

Before I go any further, I must go back to how our FA Cup campaign played out. After our epic victory over Liverpool in the third round, we were drawn at home to Burnley who we proceeded to tear apart 6-2 on a bog of a pitch, a result which only seemed to highlight the club's present fortunes – we were too good for the Second Division but the fact was that the top flight was another step up in class that we were struggling to cope with.

On my way back from Fulham Broadway that night, my imagination ran away with me. Could this be the year for our second FA Cup triumph? After all, we'd seen off Liverpool, and now Burnley, scoring ten goals over the two games. Why not, I thought. It would be just like the Blues to struggle in the league all season and then somehow manage to lift the cup on a sunny afternoon at Wembley in May.

Surely, we would overcome Second Division Orient in the fifth round. We'd had problems with the O's in the past in both league and cup games. In fact, the last time we'd faced them in the FA Cup had been at the same stage back in 1972 when we'd blown a two-goal lead at Brisbane Road to end up on the wrong end of a 3-2 scoreline. That result proved to be a seismic turning point in Chelsea's history because seven days later, we lost the League Cup Final to Stoke at Wembley. Those two exits in the space of one week were the harbinger of the dark days that were to blight the club for years as that great cup-winning side of the early 1970s was slowly broken up.

Now the difference in class between the two sides was not as wide as it was in 1972, but still, even though we'd found life in the First Division a bit of a problem, Orient, on the other hand, were not exactly setting the Second Division alight. On paper it looked like a visit to Brisbane Road would be a tricky tie, and a London derby into the bargain. But all things being equal, the prospect of another FA Cup quarter-final was there.

3

ON THE weekend of the game against Orient, I was due to go down to Trowbridge in Wiltshire for my mate Dave's first wedding anniversary. Five of us travelled down in Steve's Ford Capri (well, it was the 1970s!) For some reason, I can still recall that Nick Lowe's 'I Love the Sound of Breaking Glass' was playing on the radio as we travelled through some god-awful industrial estate in Slough. The other track I can remember being played from that journey was Althea and Donna's 'Uptown Top Ranking'. While I loved Lowe's track, I'm afraid I could have done without Althea and Donna's warbling which seemed to be on an eternal loop. Add in the fact that I still had a banging hangover from the night before when I'd spent much of the dark, lonely hours bringing up the Stella I'd been necking like it was going out of fashion, followed by the sweet 'n' sour pork balls I'd bought from a Chinese takeaway. This was common practice among me and my mates; to stuff that Chinese food which came in foil containers greedily into our mouths as we made our way home from the pub. Unfortunately, on this occasion, my constitution had said 'no thanks', resulting in my viewing the contents of my stomach for what seemed hours upon end. The other thing I can clearly recall is that it was bitterly cold, and I mean really cold. The sky was grey and overcast with the prospect of snow seeming highly likely.

When we arrived in Trowbridge we decided, like the year before, to visit the Berni Inn to have their classic '70s combo of steak and chips followed no doubt by Black Forest gâteau. By now my hangover was receding, so I decided to have a few Blue Lagoons (Cointreau, lime and lemonade) to help me on the road to recovery. During the meal some bloke of about our age – we were in our early 20s – came in with what looked like his maiden aunt. He also, unfortunately, looked like Plug out of the *Beano*, and he was wearing a tweed jacket with leather patches on the arms. Both he and his aunt looked like refugees from a bygone era. It soon became apparent that Plug had cottoned on to the fact that we were earwigging into his conversation, as he seemed to be getting more uneasy at every inane question asked of him by his aunt. It seemed to us that it was more of an incantation than a conversation, as Plug just sat there motionless while the old girl prattled on.

'Would you like breakfast in bed tomorrow, dear?' the elderly lady enquired of Plug. Before he could reply, my mate Kevin, who was never slow with a barbed comment, replied rather loudly, 'No, he'd prefer it on a plate!' which caused much hilarity on our table. Plug went bright red, unlike his aunt who looked at us with a quizzical expression on her face, which seemed to say, 'What are they laughing at?'

Looking back, it was a pretty cruel thing to do and the five of us didn't exactly cover ourselves in glory. But the alchemy of five blokes in their early 20s fuelled by drink, being given the gift of two prime targets like Plug (who seemed to have a bullseye on the back of his jacket) and his aunt (who resembled that Dickens character Miss

Havisham), well, you have the perfect blend for a concoction of merciless piss-taking.

When we arrived at Dave's I was faced with the prospect of sitting in front of the television in his front room while all my mates were secretly hoping and praying that Chelsea would get turned over by Orient. It was excruciating as updates in those days were few and far between. Every time they went back to the *Grandstand* studio, I was expecting the worst. Thankfully, I breathed a sigh of relief when the final score came through on the TV vidiprinter of Orient 0 Chelsea 0. That'll do, I thought. Now we could see them off at the Bridge.

On the evening news it was reported that Chelsea fans had been responsible for a wall collapsing behind the goal where they were massed. I remembered that the same type of thing had happened a couple of years before during our promotion season of 1976/77. It seemed that yet again, we were the culprits. The Orient chairman angrily blasted that our supporters were nothing more than thugs. Well, let me tell you, it's no wonder that bloody wall kept on collapsing because every time I came away from Brisbane Road, there was one thought that constantly went through my mind, and that was, 'What a dump!' Perhaps the aforementioned chairman should've realised that because his club's home support was meagre to say the least, it was no surprise that when the likes of Chelsea were the visitors, the said wall in its derelict state would become hazardous. But yet again, the Chelsea following was beaten with a stick in which the media seemed to take great delight. If they'd investigated a bit further, they might have noticed like I did when that wall collapsed during our 1-0 victory there in August 1976, that the edifice in question was already in a state of disrepair. In fact, it looked like it had been built using papier-mâché and cardboard. Still, let them moan, I thought. We'd got what we came for – a chance to see them off at the Bridge when surely we would capitalise on our extra class to see us through to the next round.

One thing I noticed when I saw the highlights the following day was that Chelsea were wearing sky-blue socks with a claret and white trim, alongside our normal royal blue kit. I thought it looked great but sadly to my knowledge, it was never worn again. One conclusion I've come to after all these years is that in all likelihood, they were most probably some of Orient's socks we'd borrowed because we'd overlooked that the home side wore white socks as well, which would have been considered a clash. If anyone has a definitive answer to this particular question, I'd be delighted to finally find out.

The party that night at Dave's house was a bit of a shocker. The friends of Dave's wife seemed to treat us with an air of suspicion and total indifference. As we discovered that evening, most of them worked alongside Dave's wife at the meat pie factory which turned out to be Trowbridge's main employer. Me and my mates just stood there in the front room nursing our drinks while the yokels got on with enjoying their evening. It was as though my crew ceased to exist, seemingly because they were not from around these parts. It became obvious that their mindset was that if you lived anywhere within a 25-mile radius of London, then that subsequently meant that you were nothing less than a conniving wide-boy from the Big Smoke. However, I did try on one occasion to break the ice by asking one of the most inane questions I could think of, as the girl in question hardly looked like she would be knocking on Mensa's door any time soon.

'Where do you work, then?' I enquired.

'In pies,' she answered, in a thick Wiltshire accent.

Straightaway, I came back with, 'Doesn't it get a bit hot?'

I waited for her to laugh but sadly my little attempt at humour went down like a lead balloon. She just gave me a quizzical look that said, 'What the hell is he talking about?' And consequently our conversation, which was minimal to say the least, gave up the ghost and died on the spot. We then both returned to our respective group of friends.

As that interminable night wore on, and more and more mind-numbing alcohol was consumed, I did something that I'm still haunted by to this day. Incredibly, I bet against my own beloved Blues. My mate Kevin tried to allay my fears that Chelsea would slip up in the replay against Orient. He confidently predicted that they would have no problem seeing off the O's. It was indicative of the way that outsiders, who had no interest in your team, always seemed to have 20/20 vision that cut through all the anguish and doubt you may have had about your club's fortunes.

'I don't know,' I replied. 'You never know with the cup.'

Kevin guffawed. 'You're pathetic! I'll bet you a tenner that Chelsea will win easily.'

For some strange reason, I heard myself saying, 'All right! You're on!' And we shook on the wager.

In 1978 £10 was worth a hell of a lot more than it is today. So though it was by no means a fortune, as a painter and decorator I was hardly in a position to take on this bet without some form of doubt developing in my mind. Kevin, on the other hand, was a computer analyst and had got a first in mathematics at university which meant that to him, the loss of a tenner was hardly something that was going to give him sleepless nights.

On the Saturday before the Orient replay, we'd lost 2-0 to Leeds at Elland Road. It now became clear that between now and the end of the season, Chelsea would be ensnared in an excruciating relegation dogfight. And with such a young and inexperienced team, I was hardly filled with anything approaching confidence. Still, the FA Cup was a welcome respite from our league worries, and surely a good run would lift the spirits of everyone concerned with the fortunes of Chelsea Football Club.

* * *

On the day of the replay, 27 February 1978, I decided to go on a scouting mission for records and books around Tottenham Court Road. This was made possible by the atrocious weather that day which meant that my job in the building trade was once again affected by the nefarious elements we experience in the UK on a regular basis. I set off on my journey at about three in the afternoon to begin my quest. This was a common practice in those days as in that area around Tottenham Court Road there were loads of small, independent record shops, where you could often pick up rarities. Although the records I bought that day were hardly what you would call scarce, they showed just how good the music scene was at that time.

I had bought 'Sweet Gene Vincent' by Ian Dury and the Blockheads before Christmas 1977, so it was a logical step to then purchase their debut album, *New Boots and Panties*, which turned out to be brilliant. Being an avid collector of singles, or 45s as they were known then, I bought a copy of 'Denis Denis' by Blondie. Like the rest of my mates, I'd been blown away when I saw Debbie Harry on *Top of the Pops* for the first time. I remember phoning a couple of my mates to ask them if they'd seen her. There's no doubt she was incredible to look at and had the right kind of swagger and attitude that perfectly summed up the new wave of music that was just breaking through in those days. I also managed to find a copy of 'Journey' by Duncan Browne which I'd been searching for since 1972, and then found the

Eddie and the Hot Rods single, 'Quit This Town', which I actually preferred to their biggest hit, 'Do Anything You Wanna Do'. I'd seen Eddie and the Hot Rods at the Hemel Pavilion with support act Squeeze, whose debut single, 'Take Me, I'm Yours', had been a minor hit recently.

Jools Holland was still in the band at that time – a band that would go on to provide two of England's finest ever writers of intelligent, sardonic pop music, namely Glenn Tilbrook and Chris Difford. If I remember correctly, the other band on that night were the Radio Stars, who'd had some chart success with their single 'Nervous Wreck', a record that I'd bought on the same day as I purchased 'Drummer Man' by Tonight. Both of these bands were among many who fell into the category of faux new wave, so consequently, being a Costello devotee, the acquisition of these two singles was not something I was ever going to shout from the rooftops.

Perhaps the best two examples of people trying to cash in on new wave at that time were Plastic Bertrand's 'Sa Plane Pour Moi', which was a hit that summer, and The Jags' 'Back of my Hand', which followed a year later in the summer of 1979. The latter, in truth, was a brilliant pastiche of my hero, Elvis Costello, and though The Jags were castigated for ripping off the Costello and the Attractions' sound, I have to admit, I loved it. All in all, that was a great era for music, one which I fear will sadly, never ever be repeated.

Being a bookworm since childhood, I was also searching all of the little bookshops situated around Shaftesbury Avenue and bought *The Collected Works of Edgar Allan Poe* (nice, light reading) and a few Jules Verne novels which I loved. Books have always been a passion for me, and I've not been without one to read since I read *All Quiet on the Western Front* when I was 12 years old.

After having something to eat in a Wimpy, which included my favourite dessert, the Brown Derby, I started out on my journey to the Bridge. Talking about Wimpy, although they were derided as nothing more than a pale imitation of the American burger joints, I personally loved them. The big joke around them in those days was when it was announced in the TV adverts, 'Why not walk into a Wimpy today?' an invitation that was turned on its head by all the smart-arses into, 'Walk into a Wimpy? I'd rather walk into a lamppost!'

The weather that night, as I've already mentioned, was awful but despite the rain and the biting wind, there was still a crowd of just over 30,000 at the Bridge. I took up my usual position in front of the tea bar next to the West Stand benches for what I hoped would be a routine victory over a lower-division side, a result that would give us a place in the last eight of the FA Cup. There was a late change in the Chelsea starting line-up as Ray Lewington came in for Kenny Swain. As we later discovered, Lewington was drafted in because Swain had failed to turn up in time for the team talk. It's a good job that the Chelsea faithful were not aware of this as it would hardly have filled anyone with confidence that we could get a result that night. Such a laissez-faire attitude would not have been tolerated by the ex-boss, the sadly missed Eddie McCreadie. Under his stewardship there was certainly no doubt as to who was in charge, but it seems that the more placid Ken Shellito had created a culture whereupon players could come and go as they pleased. Swain's tardiness was punished by nothing more than a paltry fine whereas Eddie Mac in all likelihood would have hung the errant striker from one of the Bridge's floodlight pylons for such an act of disrespect. Don't get me wrong, I really rated Kenny Swain. He had proven himself to be a clever inside-forward since he broke into the first team in 1974, especially in the promotion season of 1976/77 when he formed an exciting strike partnership with Steve Finnieston which made this sorry episode even more disappointing, that a senior pro actually thought that it was acceptable to turn up late.

Swain went on to have a great career when he left Stamford Bridge for Aston Villa, where he was converted into a full-back and went on to win the First Division in 1981, followed the year after by even more glory was bestowed on Swain as he was a member of the Villa side that overcame Bayern Munich in the European Cup Final. If somebody had told me that night just what a career Swain was going to enjoy once he'd rescued himself from a club that was going nowhere fast, I doubt if I would have believed them.

Chelsea seemed to be controlling things against Orient and all seemed to be going to plan when O's defender Billy Roffey panicked and sent his lobbed back pass over the head of goalkeeper John Jackson straight into the back of the Shed goal. Though Chelsea had not played with the style and elan they'd produced during the two previous rounds, when they'd wiped the floor with both Liverpool and Burnley, they still looked really comfortable and went in at the break with that one-goal advantage. On that bitterly cold and damp evening, like so many on the terraces around me, I couldn't stop myself dreaming of a place in the last eight where if we prevailed, we'd face Middlesbrough at Ayresome Park which would be another winnable tie, a prospect which would mean a place in the semi-finals of the FA Cup, something we hadn't achieved for eight long years. Yet, once again like so many Blues fans there that night who'd seen our club snatch defeat from the jaws of victory on countless occasions, we were quite aware that the next

45 minutes would be far from easy. The next goal would be pivotal – a second for Chelsea would surely mean the end of Orient's cup dreams. There was an air of inevitability when the prospect of Orient equalising became a stark reality with Peter Kitchen levelling the score four minutes after the break. In that moment the game swung on its axis. Suddenly Orient started to dominate possession and looked threatening every time they came forward. Chelsea on the other hand looked bereft of ideas and the whole team resembled nothing more than a balloon that had burst, their confidence draining out right before the Blues faithful's worried glare.

There's a feeling in football that suddenly pervades you at the realisation that this is not going to be your day, a sickening premonition in the pit of your stomach that it is only a matter of time before the worst happens. That dread almost felt like the Sword of Damocles hanging over our heads. In the 74th minute, Kitchen scored a fine solo goal as he went past several Chelsea defenders to put Orient 2-1 up. There was an eerie silence around the Bridge as the ball hit the back of Peter Bonetti's net, which was only disturbed by the Orient away support celebrating at the North End. Though Chelsea applied pressure on the O's defence, sadly there was no breakthrough and consequently the Blues' one chance of redemption that season disappeared into that cold February night. It was hard to take in just what had happened during the last 90 minutes but the cold, hard facts were that once again we were out of the cup. Sadly, it all seemed to be a very Chelsea thing to do – put in a sparkling display at the Bridge to beat the mighty Liverpool, who went on to retain the European Cup later that season, only to turn in a listless surrender to Orient who were struggling in the lower reaches of the Second Division. As it turned out, Orient beat Middlesbrough in a replay at Brisbane

Road before losing 3-0 to Arsenal in the semi-final, which was played at Stamford Bridge of all places.

What strange coincidences football can sometimes throw up because for a couple of years both of the sides who'd knocked us out of the FA Cup at the fifth-round stage, who were in a lower division, went on to reach the last four at the Bridge, a fact that doesn't upset me one iota. So, hard luck, Crystal Palace and Orient. Though you managed to end my beloved Blues' interest in the most important cup competition at the time, your celebrating and gloating at the end of the day, came to precisely nothing. Amen.

* * *

While travelling back from Fulham Broadway with the records and books I'd bought earlier in the day, I must have cut a lonely figure in my donkey jacket, and my red, white, and green away scarf that I still have to this day. Like many other Chelsea supporters at the replay, I was now looking with some concern at the upcoming fixtures. After that performance it now seemed that between now and the end of the season, the Blues would indeed have their work cut out to ensure that they wouldn't be making a swift return to the Second Division, which we'd found so difficult to get out of the previous year. Thankfully, it only took three wins from our remaining fixtures to achieve safety.

As I mentioned previously, on the Saturday after the Orient capitulation, Chelsea somehow contrived to murder Liverpool again at the Bridge with another blistering display that made our cup exit a few days earlier even more difficult to comprehend. Further victories at Leicester, who were already relegated, and at home to local rivals QPR, made sure that the Blues retained their First Division status for one more season at least. The downside was that in those remaining fixtures we'd also managed to lose six games, including a humiliating 6-0 reverse against Everton at Goodison Park.

Those last few weeks of the season were nothing short of torture. I can clearly remember the home game against Wolves, who were themselves in the relegation scrap. Watching that match was not good for one's mental health as Chelsea defended an early lead right up to the last few minutes before Wolves sickeningly equalised. It was a horrendous blow to our chances of avoiding the drop but could have been so much worse if the referee hadn't disallowed a Wolves goal which seemed to be extremely hard on the visitors. When the final table was tallied up the Blues had finished in 16th place, four points clear of West Ham, who hysterically joined Newcastle and Leicester in the bottom three relegation places. I, for one, was ecstatic at West Ham's failure. Their 3-1 win against us in March at the end of the day had counted for nothing. Revenge, as they say, is a dish best served cold.

On the Friday night after the FA Cup exit to Orient, me and my mates made our way to the local boozer. When we got to the bar, my mate Kevin said, 'Oh, by the way, before I forget,' and promptly handed me a tenner.

'What's this?' I enquired.

'Our bet,' Kevin said. It then dawned on me about the wager we had made when we were at that party in Wiltshire. Here it was, my blood money, my reward for betting against my own team. At that moment I felt unclean, as though it had been personally my fault that Chelsea had been knocked out of the cup. Somehow it was all down to me. I was nothing but a faithless excuse of a man. I'd like to say that I refused the money, but sadly that was not the case and after all, it was a tenner. And why shouldn't I get something out of what had been a miserable episode? Anyway, I thought, Kevin had goaded me into taking the bet by his supreme belief that victory over Orient would be nothing more than a formality. Still, all these years later, I have to hold my hands up. It was unforgivable and it's something I've never repeated.

Later that year, though I've in no way ever been a gambler, I took a bet on the Netherlands to win the 1978 World Cup in Argentina as the local bookies had them at longer odds than bloody Scotland. I can't remember what the odds were, but I know that if Rob Rensenbrink's shot in the closing minutes of the final had gone in instead of hitting the post, I'd have been £150 better off – a lot of money in those days. Perhaps in a way, this was my punishment for betting against my own team just a few months earlier.

The driving force about my decision to lay money on the Dutch was the fact that even the bookmakers were buying into all of the hyperbole about Ally's Tartan Army. Unbelievably, these arrogant, deluded Scots had actually posed with a replica of football's ultimate prize before the tournament had even kicked off. In an extreme display of hubris, manager Ally MacLeod and his squad of eternal optimists even went as far as going on an open-top bus parade around Hampden Park, much to the delight of the half-crazed, or more likely totally inebriated, tartan hordes who willingly took part in this embarrassing fiasco. It seemed that the madness had also permeated into the mind of Rod Stewart, who despite being born in London, was not slow in telling anyone who was interested that his loyalty definitely lay north of the border – a tartan scarf being the defining image of poor old Rod the Mod. It seemed that one of his parents had Scottish links and this planted the seed in Rod's head that the bullshit and bluster of the Highland mob was preferable to facing up to the truth that he was English, after all.

Rod, in his infinite wisdom, decided to record his own contribution to Scotland's World Cup adventure in the execrable 'Ole, Ola' which was every bit as awful as it sounds. As far as I can remember, Rod was warbling in his raspy voice those immortal words of the chorus, 'Ole, Ola, We're Gonna Win the World Cup, over thar,' which must be one of the worst couplets inflicted on the record-buying public. Don't get me wrong, I loved Rod Stewart's early stuff and had the albums, *Never a Dull Moment* and *Every Picture Tells a Story*, but to go from releasing such classics as 'Maggie May' and 'You Wear It Well' just a few years previously, to this steaming turd, was nothing short of taking the piss. Oh, before I finish, if you weren't aware, Scotland came home after failing to qualify from their group – an honour they still hold to this day as they are the only home nation who have never qualified for the knockout stages of a major international competition. And this is a sad indictment of a nation who are never slow at blowing their own trumpet. So, just remember, any time you get the chance to burst their balloon of self-delusion, my advice is to act upon it for the greater good of all humanity.

* * *

One more strange episode occurred towards the end of Chelsea's first season back in the top flight. You will recall my earlier mention about the meal me and my mates went to in Trowbridge in January 1978 where we sat opposite Plug and his maiden aunt and the rather unkind comments that passed from our callow, youthful lips, an episode which in all honesty was best forgotten. That was until one of my friends, Chris, enquired one evening after five-a-sides if any of us could shed some light on what had occurred regarding his overcoat. I, like the rest of us, wondered what the hell he was talking about. Chris then proceeded to enlighten us. It seemed that since the weather had turned warmer after our visit to Trowbridge on that bitterly cold February day, the overcoat that had been worn by Chris was consigned to his wardrobe, there to remain during the spring and summer months until the weather turned cold again. In all honesty, none of us had a clue what he was going on about.

We soon got our answer. Chris explained that a strange smell was coming from his wardrobe, a stench that had begun to upset his mother every time she made his bed. Back in those days, this was seen as a woman's job which highlighted the spoilt attitude of my generation who still required their mummy to clear up after them. After some investigation, Chris's mum found exactly where the rancid odour was permeating from. It was, as you've most probably suspected, coming from Chris's overcoat. Upon closer inspection she found a rotting piece of meat wrapped in a napkin in one of the coat pockets. She was very house-proud to put it mildly, and her reaction to discovering this monstrosity was one of extreme revulsion. When Chris returned home from work that day, she asked him what the hell was going on and how dare he leave his rotting leftovers in her pristine house. Chris pleaded both innocence and ignorance of how this stinking piece of meat had ended up in said pocket. When Chris took a closer look at the napkin, he saw that it belonged to the chain of restaurants where we had dined in Trowbridge. Chris quickly worked out that there could only be three suspects: Kevin, Mick and myself. He then proceeded to question the three of us, 'Which of you idiots would do such a thing?'

You would have thought that there would have been protestations of innocence from his three dining companions. You'd be wrong because unbelievably, Mick piped up straightaway, and said, 'That was me.'

To say that the rest of us were incredulous is an understatement. There was a stunned silence that was only broken by Chris enquiring, 'What the hell was he playing at!'

'Well,' Mick replied, 'that bit of meat was a bit gristly, so I decided to get rid of it.' Unbelievably, it seemed that Mick thought his moment of madness was something that could, after all, be justified.

'Why didn't you leave it on your plate?' Chris finally bellowed.

'Well,' Mick said, 'your coat was on the back of your chair, and it seemed easier to deposit it there.'

To this day, I can offer no explanation for Mick's act of insanity, and I'm sure, neither can he. Mick had a degree in physics from Reading University, which only goes to prove that walking the halls of academia in no way helps you to learn the social etiquette of life. And so the curtain came down on 'meat-gate'.

The curtain also came down on Chelsea's 1977/78 campaign. It had been a tremendous relief that the club had survived that inaugural season back in the hardest league in the land. Yet it was obvious that unless some additions were made to the team during the summer months, then the new season was again likely to prove just as arduous as the previous one. The only problem was that Chelsea were, in a word, broke, which led many Blues fans to see the summer of 1978 as nothing more than a stay of execution before the inevitable happened. Yet no one was prepared for just how far the club would fall that following year because 1978/79 was the most nightmarish experience Chelsea had ever suffered in their history. Of course the Blues, not content with putting their followers through the mangle once, managed to nearly top it in the calamitous 1982/83 campaign. But more of that later.

4

WHEN THE fixtures were announced for the new season, I was away on a lads' holiday in the Isle of Wight. That was the umpteenth time that I'd visited the island, where I now live. For some reason the Isle of Wight had a magnetic attraction for myself and my mates. While scanning the opening fixtures in the newspaper, my mate Kevin asked me politely, 'Be honest, how many points do you think Chelsea are going to get with that team you've got?' After my indignation had subsided that a Watford supporter should question my beloved Blues (seeing that he supported a team that had never come close to playing in the top flight), I proceeded to scan the newspaper for Chelsea's fixture list. I tried to be as objective as I could and just looked at the cold, hard reality of the opponents we would be facing in the upcoming campaign. Depressingly, and with a startling clarity of vision, I predicted a total which was just four more points than we actually managed in that train wreck of a season.

It's hard to comprehend for Chelsea supporters these days who've been brought up on 20 years of unparalleled success with a whole host of marquee signings, that by the closing days of the summer of 1978 Chelsea had not bought one single new player. Since David Hay and John Sissons arrived at the Bridge four years earlier (yes, that's right, four long years), between 1974 and 1978 the Blues had failed to add one new face to the first-team squad. That, and the money that had been poured into the East Stand, were two very good reasons as to why the club was in such a parlous state on and off the field.

Myself and thousands of other Blues fans could only stand and enviously watch on as our opponents constantly strengthened their sides. With Chelsea now cast firmly in the role of paupers, we had no choice but to rely on youngsters coming through the youth system to keep the club afloat. Of all these prospects, it was only the supremely talented Ray Wilkins who was of a standard that compared to the brilliant generation of the 1960s when the club had produced Peter Osgood, John Hollins and Peter Bonetti, and of course before them we had unearthed the gem that was the mercurial Jimmy Greaves, who broke into the Chelsea side back in 1957 when he scored a brilliant debut goal against Spurs at White Hart Lane. Incredible to think that he was only 17 years old that day. From the rest of Eddie Mac's promotion-winning side of 1976/77, some of the players went on to have really decent careers but unfortunately for the Blues, it was usually with other clubs who cherry-picked our prize assets almost at will. Already the growing consensus was that if we struggled in the forthcoming campaign then that would surely result in the loss of our talisman Wilkins.

After the Blues had lost to Everton on the opening day of the season, they travelled to Molineux to face Wolves in midweek and came away with a 1-0 victory which, to be honest, was a bit of a surprise. I'd hoped that Tommy Langley's winner would put us in the right frame of mind to face our next opponents, the old enemy Spurs at White Hart Lane. Spurs were now back in the top division after crashing down into the second tier the year before. Very quickly they showed their intent to make a mark back in the top flight by signing Argentine internationals Osvaldo Ardiles and Ricky Villa, who'd both featured in their country's World Cup-winning side that summer. To be fair, it was Ardiles who caught the eye and imagination of the footballing public in this country, as he'd been a first choice, whereas Villa had been pretty much nothing more than a bystander during the tournament.

It was a brilliant sunny afternoon at White Hart Lane and to my surprise, and I should imagine also to the surprise of the vast away support that day, Chelsea took the field in a most unfamiliar kit of yellow shirts with green trim, green shorts, and yellow socks. It looked fantastic, even though it bore a striking resemblance to the colours worn by our country cousins from Norfolk, Norwich. Trust Chelsea, I thought. No matter what state the club is in you could always rely on the Blues to consistently come up with some striking kits in those days. For instance, previously we'd been the first side to wear the combination of yellow shirts, blue shorts, and yellow socks as our away strip back in the mid-1960s, which led to the world and his wife following our initiative by wearing the same kit, including Arsenal and Spurs, much to my horror. And it didn't stop there. Leeds and Everton and even West Brom followed suit but as they say, imitation is the sincerest form of flattery.

Despite the ticker-tape welcome for Spurs from their dubious home support, a trend that had started during that summer's World Cup, Chelsea went toe-to-toe with the north Londoners that day and a Kenny Swain brace earned us a creditable 2-2 draw. What I found hysterical was that every time Spurs scored, within 60 seconds their fans' cheers were choked off in the back of their throats as Chelsea instantly struck back. A few weeks later, Ardiles and Villa and the rest of the Spurs mob got a taste of what life was all about in the top flight when they were torn to pieces by Liverpool at Anfield who hit seven past them without reply. I actually knew a Spurs supporter who went to that game. He used to drink at our local. According to him, some fans actually started to cry as Liverpool put them to the sword. My joy at this result was somewhat curtailed as it was becoming patently obvious that Chelsea were destined for another season of struggle.

Around the time of the 3-0 home defeat against Leeds, always a bitter pill to swallow, I read a newspaper headline which stated 'Chelsea Swoop for Duncan'. What the hell, I thought, four years without buying one single player and now we're trying to sign a Tottenham reject, their misfiring centre-forward John Duncan. But as I looked closer, I realised it was in fact the maverick Duncan McKenzie of Everton who we were interested in. McKenzie was a bit of a loose cannon, but without doubt, he was a highly gifted crowd-pleaser, something that the Blues had been crying out for since the departure of Ossie. The saga of whether Chelsea would sign McKenzie dragged on and on for a couple of weeks. Every day I would scan the papers for any updates on the situation; both morning and evening editions were purchased to see if there was any progress in negotiations. You've got to understand that when your club hasn't bought anybody for years, the news that we were prepared to pay Everton £175,000 for McKenzie's signature was seen as an event of seismic proportions for the Stamford Bridge faithful.

At one stage it seemed that the deal was off. I was devastated and, as it happens, so were the Chelsea hierarchy. Brian Mears, the chairman, sadly announced, 'It's a sad day for the club, that negotiations have broken down with the player failing to agree terms.' So, it seemed after all, that the transfer wasn't happening. I was gutted. Then out of nowhere, the news broke that terms had now been agreed between player and club and that McKenzie would soon be wearing the blue shirt of Chelsea. I was overjoyed and so was Kevin. Being a Watford supporter, he had no interest in Chelsea's fortunes and was sick to the stomach of me asking him the question every five minutes or so on whether McKenzie would sign for the Blues.

'If I never hear that bugger's name again, I'll be highly delighted!' was Kevin's scathing comment about our new signing. In truth, I was quite aware that I was slowly driving him mad but by this stage, any bit of news that brightened up the prospects of a club that had been in terrible decline for ages was indeed something to shout about. Kevin, on the other hand, was growing increasingly cocky about Watford, who were just starting out on the most successful period in their history. Around about that time, Watford had knocked Manchester United out of the League Cup at Old Trafford, a result I found hard to take because as far as I was concerned, Watford had been nothing more than a joke when I'd started going down the fields to play football with my mates in 1970. Whereas I supported one of the most successful and glamorous sides in the country, Watford were just a struggling Second Division outfit. But since Elton John started splashing some of his vast fortune on the club that he'd supported all of his life, their rise had been meteoric. What made it worse was that this was a period when the Blues' fortunes started plummeting in the opposite direction. I'm pleased to say that today, normal service has been resumed and once again, Chelsea dine at the top table of the game again while Watford are left, once more, to feed off the scraps.

* * *

After our draw at White Hart Lane, it came as no surprise to anyone who might have read my previous books that I then went on holiday, yet again, to the Isle of Wight. The B&B that Kevin and I were staying at was your typical run-of-the-mill place that was only saved from disappearing into the recesses of my memory by the strange case of Buddy Love. Buddy, as we called him, was a teenager who bore a striking resemblance to the character that Jerry Lewis portrayed in that classic comedy, *The Nutty Professor*. I hasten to add that it wasn't the smooth-talking ladies' man the professor turned into when he drank the magic potion that somehow turned him from a complete dork into a suave, piano-playing charmer. I'm afraid this poor sod did indeed have the pudding bowl haircut, buck teeth, and pebble glasses that Lewis had donned in the film. Much to Kevin's amusement, he'd noticed that Buddy used to come to the breakfast table with his mum and dad every morning wearing a Chelsea pendant around his neck. He was also clutching a Chelsea annual. In fact, I never saw him without it. Subsequently, because Buddy was a fellow Chelsea fan, Kevin used this as a stick to beat me with, suggesting at every mealtime, 'Why don't you go and say hello to your fellow supporter? I'm sure he'd be interested to talk Chelsea with you.'

'Just leave it, Kev,' was my desperate reply, a reaction that Kevin found highly amusing.

Buddy's parents were an odd couple to say the least. As far as I can recall, his mum never uttered a word during the whole time they were down there. She'd just mutely sit there picking at her food like a distressed sparrow. Buddy was fairly tall, not far off six feet. The father, however, was somewhat, shall we say, vertically challenged. He seemed to affect a weariness every time Buddy would ask him the incessant questions he subjected his dad to every mealtime.

His father also wore a rather strange jacket that looked suspiciously like a bus driver's uniform, complete with piping on the collar and stripes around the cuffs. It was only later in the week that me and Kevin had our theory confirmed when we both clocked that the bus company badge had been removed but had still left that indelible mark, and that Buddy's old man had indeed once been behind the wheel of the number 37 to the cemetery gates. I've often wondered whatever happened to Buddy and how he coped with later life. I realise that me and Kevin were incredibly cruel in our attitude towards somebody who was somehow different to what we considered to be normal. In our defence, I submit the fact that we were both in our early 20s, an age when consideration and understanding are often in short supply in young men. Years later, older, and wiser, I hope, I can see his parents' world in a different light, one of compassion and understanding.

* * *

I'm sure I wasn't alone in viewing Chelsea's 1978/79 campaign in pretty much the same way as all Blues fans – an unmitigated disaster. It soon became patently obvious that the team was just not good enough as defeat followed defeat. The saviour that we hoped for in our new signing, Duncan McKenzie, turned out to be nothing short of a nightmare. Though he scored on his debut in a 3-2 defeat to Coventry, and another effort against the club who sold him, Everton, he only managed four goals for the club, all sadly away from home, before he was binned out in the new year as surplus to requirements. After all that hope that McKenzie might be our salvation, he turned out in the end to be exactly what he was: a skilful player of undoubted quality who was most effective in a team that had players around him who would do his running for him, allowing

McKenzie to display his vast array of flicks and tricks. Sadly, that was a luxury that this young, struggling Chelsea side had no use for.

The one bright spot that autumn was an incredible 4-3 victory over Bolton Wanderers at the Bridge. At one stage Chelsea had been trailing 3-0 and although Tommy Langley pulled a goal back in the seventy-second minute for the Blues, that scoreline remained the same until five minutes before the final whistle, My God was I tempted to leave my place in front of the tea bar as yet another humiliation seemed to be very much on the cards. That was until the mercurial Clive Walker took the game by the scruff of the neck and carved Bolton's tiring defence to pieces. Within minutes, Chelsea had pulled back the three-goal deficit and were now searching for the unlikeliest of winners. Once again Walker ran at the visitors' defence, which by this time looked totally shell-shocked, a panic that led to Big Sam Allardyce turning Walker's low cross from the left wing into his own net at the Shed end. There was absolute pandemonium all around me as the Chelsea fans, who'd had very little to cheer about that season, celebrated like we'd just won the Champions League. Sadly it was a flame that flickered briefly and then miserably died away.

It's hard to explain to the newbies who support the Blues and have only known success in their short time on this planet just how appalling it was around this time at the Bridge. Now I read tweets from young Chelsea fans who are devastated if a result goes against us, spitting their bile and invective on any player or manager who takes their fancy. I've also noticed an air of impatience at the Bridge if Chelsea fail to score in the first 20 minutes or so. A way of intolerance that smacks of very little knowledge regarding the game from these plastic fans who, to all intents and purposes, are nothing more than glorified tourists.

As if things couldn't get worse that year, the board in their infinite wisdom decided a different manager might change the club's fortunes. There were rumours that Miljan Miljanić, the Yugoslav national team boss, might take over from the now departed Ken Shellito. But, of course, these rumours came to precisely nothing as did the exciting news that the Blues were interested in signing the world-class talent by the name of Johan Cruyff, the Dutch maestro, who was now playing for New York Cosmos and had featured in a 1-1 draw at the Bridge in a charity game. It seemed far-fetched and, in a word, incredulous, that our club in such a perilous state would be able to attract one of the greatest players of all time, persuading him to give up a comfortable, well-paid life in the USA for a relegation struggle with a club that had the word 'doomed' attached to it. Yet again, those rumours turned out to be just that – rumours – and it soon became patently obvious that Cruyff was indeed going nowhere.

Still, there was a lot of young managerial talent out there. Terry Venables would have been a prime candidate. As an ex-player he knew the club inside out. Chelsea had already had success when appointing Eddie Mac, another former Stamford Bridge star, but this being the Blues, chairman Brian Mears and his cohorts chose a left-field option when the board appointed the Double-winning Spurs captain Danny Blanchflower. It's true that in his time he'd been one of the most gifted midfield players this country had ever seen. But Blanchflower had no experience of managing in club football. He had in fact been plying his trade since his retirement from the game as a very successful journalist. One can only imagine that poor old Danny was the last one out of the room as the stampede headed for the exit door after Mears posed the question, 'Any volunteers?' It was without doubt a ludicrous appointment.

Blanchflower was totally out of touch with the modern game. Yes, he was a dry-witted, intelligent commentator, but managing and writing are very different sides of the same coin. He was the archetypal Irishman, full of the old blarney. Predictably, this appointment was a total disaster in an era of abject misery.

Stories have emerged that Blanchflower had very little interest in taking training sessions. He was quite content, it seemed, to give the first-team squad a quick pep talk before heading off in a cloud of dust as his car sped away for his appointment at the golf club. Honestly, you couldn't make it up. In an air of sheer desperation, Blanchflower brought prodigal son and club legend Peter Osgood back to the Bridge, a move that turned out to be nothing more than a prime example of why you should never, ever, retrace your own footsteps. Ossie's first goal back came in a 7-2 humiliation at Ayresome Park against Middlesbrough, who were managed that day by a certain John Neal, but more of him later.

By now, Duncan McKenzie had practically disappeared from the line-up. It was obvious that Blanchflower didn't fancy him. In all honesty, McKenzie's form had been erratic, and matters weren't helped when the player declared in the national press that he'd failed to settle in London and a move might be the best thing for both parties. In the end McKenzie got his wish and left the Blues, scoring just four goals in 15 league appearances. All of McKenzie's goalscoring efforts came away from home, the last being in the shock 3-2 victory over Manchester City at Maine Road. It was also the last time Ossie would score for the club, as his return petered out into nothing more than a rather sad footnote. That win at Maine Road is largely remembered for Clive Walker's brilliant individual goal which secured the points. Indeed, it is an enduring image that still lives on in the memories of supporters of a certain vintage as Walker, in the yellow and green away strip, bore down on the City goal, orange ball at his feet, gliding over the snow-covered pitch to complete a fine breakaway move for the winning strike. Unhappily, I also remember that game for something that happened the following week.

At that time there was a chat show on ITV hosted by Eamonn Andrews. While old Eamonn was perfectly at home on that long-running institution, *This is Your Life*, he was execrable as a chat show host and seemed to be in a constant state of apoplexy, with sweat streaming down his face which consequently managed to make his guests feel just as ill at ease as he so obviously was.

Not to put too fine a point on it, the show was a complete and utter train wreck – Michael Parkinson, he most definitely was not. Anyway, one of the guests on Eamonn's show that week was none other than Manchester City manger Malcolm Allison. I should imagine when Big Mal agreed to appear on this show, he would have thought that a home game against rock-bottom Chelsea would hardly be any cause for concern, but to his horror he now had to appear before the unflinching cameras and somehow explain away what had been a catastrophic and humiliating defeat. Good old Eamonn didn't spare him one iota, saying, 'What happened then, Mal?'

Before the embarrassed Allison could offer any excuses, Eamonn said, 'OK, let's take a look at the goals from Saturday.'

They then proceeded to show the highlights from the game and then cut back to Big Mal, whose hands were covering his face in acute shame. The audience and all the other guests were laughing their heads off at Allison's toe-curling humiliation. So it had come to this; the fact that

Allison's side had lost to Chelsea was viewed as nothing more than a cue for huge merriment. Once again, Chelsea, who had tried for years to rid themselves of being the butt of every music hall comedian, now found themselves viewed as nothing more than a joke.

I'd had a few drinks before watching that programme and I can clearly recall that it was a freezing-cold January night. In my naivety, I thought it would be entertaining to watch Big Mal squirming in front of the watching TV audience. Not for one minute did I expect Chelsea to be included in his public pillorying. But there it was, leaving me and every Blues fan watching that night with the unthinkable reality that Chelsea were seen by the great British public as something to be ridiculed. After the effects of the alcohol had dissipated in me, I realised in a split second that week in, week out, I would have to go out on a Saturday night to be met by a wall of derision and sarcasm from my gloating mates, after Chelsea had suffered yet another coating. It seemed as though this awful season would never come to an end.

* * *

I can remember one Saturday when Chelsea's game was postponed due to arctic conditions. I believe it was against Nottingham Forest at the City Ground. I can recall making my way to the pub with a feeling of elation that for one night at least, I'd be spared the barbed, biting comments from my mates about yet another calamitous performance. It's a good job that I made the most of that reprieve. A few weeks later, the rearranged fixture was played and with a cruel inevitability, Forest put the hapless Blues to the sword, scoring six goals without reply. Shortly after this, Brian Clough's men visited the Bridge for the return match. After taking the lead, once again the Blues fell apart and

Forest ran out comfortable 3-1 winners. By now, of course, everyone connected with Chelsea had come to the sad conclusion that relegation was no longer a possibility – it was a nailed-on certainty.

Another match I can remember with sickening clarity is the 5-1 thrashing the Blues were on the end of when we played Ipswich at Portman Road. The gulf in class between the two sides was, in a word, alarming. It was difficult to accept that a small, provincial club like Ipswich, who only a few years ago I would have considered to be no more than a collection of country bumpkins, were now lording it over my club, whose fall from grace had been both swift and shocking.

After the 2-1 home victory over Birmingham City on 3 February when Ray Wilkins secured the points for the Blues with a 20-yard piledriver in front of the Shed, there was to be only one more home win that season. That came against Middlesbrough, when relegation had already been confirmed, making this a match of total insignificance, apart from the fact that Wilkins's brother Graham netted his one and only goal for the Blues. During his Chelsea career he also netted a few at the wrong end including a howler at Bolton in 1976 and, who could forget his last-minute aberration that gave West Ham a 1-0 win at the Bridge in September 1980?

Relegation had already been confirmed over Easter that year when Arsenal delivered the *coup de grâce* at Highbury when they ran out easy 5-2 winners. Along with many of the Chelsea faithful, I was somewhat relieved when it had finally become fact that once again, we were indeed, the boys in blue from Division Two. Better to play in a division in which we had a chance than the nightmare we'd endured in the 1978/79 campaign where pitiful performances against superior opponents had become endemic.

There had been a bit of movement in the transfer market during that hellish season. Kenny Swain, who'd been so impressive during our promotion campaign of 1976/77, was allowed to leave for Aston Villa after it became apparent that he was unsettled and craved top-flight football. The other bit of business Chelsea were involved in was the arrival of Eamonn Bannon from the Scottish club Hearts in early 1979. It was the last signing of the beleaguered Danny Blanchflower, a deal that proved so unsuccessful that, incredibly, Bannon was the first one out of the door when Geoff Hurst replaced Blanchflower later that year.

Another victim of Hurst's sweeping of the new broom was that Ossie was ousted from the Bridge. Apparently it seemed that there was no room for any other hero at the club. Perhaps not the wisest of moves on Hurst's part was the removal of a legend who to this day is still regarded as the King of Stamford Bridge. In my opinion Hurst's treatment of Ossie was a bit rich due to the fact that Hurst as a player was not fit to lace his boots. And I believe he took some delight in shoving Ossie through the door as some sort of proof that he had won what seemed to be a rather pathetic power struggle.

When Glenn Hoddle took over the manager's seat in 1993, it was reported that he took great delight in showing his squad of bang-average players that he had not lost any of his graceful talent, and lost patience with them when they could not reproduce the tricks and flicks that he was famous for. Ex-Blue Tony Cascarino said in his book, 'If Hoddle was made of chocolate, he'd eat himself,' which led to anger and resentment among the players who had not been blessed with his God-given talent.

As you can gather, I wasn't exactly overjoyed when Hurst took over from poor old befuddled Blanchflower. I was even less impressed when the monkey-faced Bobby Gould was named as his assistant. As a player, especially for Arsenal, I had loathed Gould. If anyone was more deserving of being given the mother of all right-handers that Leeds keeper Gary Sprake dished out to him, I've yet to see it. Gould, at best, was an honest, hard-working grafter of limited ability. He was also full of it, and just couldn't seem to keep his trap shut, a habit he carried on into his managerial career. He remains one of the most manic pundits ever inflicted on the listening public during his time at talkSPORT. I have a strong suspicion that Hurst's main reason for appointing Gould was not for his tactical ability, but for his loud mouth which would hopefully keep the troops in order. Still, now Hurst was the man in charge, and as long as he was at the helm, supporters would give him our full backing, if somewhat begrudgingly.

It's hard to believe in this day and age that this was Hurst's first managerial job in professional football. His only experience up to that point had been in charge of non-league Telford United. Hardly a ringing endorsement considering the task he had on his hands in trying to take the Blues back to the top flight. And so the curtain came down on what must be one of the worst campaigns in the club's history. The final two games against Arsenal at the Bridge, and Manchester United at Old Trafford, perversely brought about two of our best results that season, with the Blues managing credible 1-1 draws against that year's FA Cup finalists. The fact that both teams probably had their minds on their Wembley date explains the reason why both of our opponents seemed distracted and fielded some of their fringe players. That allowed us to take two points which in turn elevated our total for the season to the grand total of just 20 points. Yes, that's right – 20 points.

I know it's hard to comprehend. The craving for instant success has now taken on such ridiculous proportions that even the lower-league clubs hire and fire managers on a regular basis, so much so that the manager's door to his office has now been replaced by a turnstile for easier access as the next poor sap takes his place in the still warm, hot seat. I must say that Sky Sports are one of the main culprits of this absurd merry-go-round. Their lurid, hyperbolic reporting of transfers and managerial sackings is, in a word, tiresome. And don't get me started on their viewers' polls they continually run; subjects like, should so-and-so sign some obscure player that you've never heard of? I for one, couldn't care less. The only thing that captures my interest is who is playing for Chelsea in the next game and whether we win it. End of.

5

SOMETIMES, I long for the days when the game of football was just *Match of the Day* on Saturday, and ITV's *The Big Match* on a Sunday, when you actually had to go to the games in order to have a valid opinion. Nowadays the world is full of armchair experts who've never seen the inside of a football stadium. I used to enjoy someone remarking to me that Chelsea hadn't done well that week, whereupon I would snap back, 'Did you go to the game?' The answer was almost always in the negative, allowing me to bite back with, 'Well, I did. So, what the fuck do you know?'

Our last home game of that terrible 1978/79 season was the 1-1 draw against Arsenal, a match that would have slipped into the mists of time as being instantly forgettable. Apart from one thing, that is. Because it saw the final Chelsea appearance of legendary goalkeeper Peter Bonetti. After 20 years of service, it was somewhat sad and poignant that the Cat's career, which had been so full of highs, should come to an end in what was one of the bleakest eras that the club had ever endured. Yet another member of the iconic early 1970s side had disappeared into the ether. Bonetti had hardly played that season and was replaced by the exciting if somewhat erratic Peter Borata, who was not in the class of his predecessor. It would be another four years before we managed to replace the Cat with someone who would come close to being considered as being mentioned in the same breath, when Welsh international Eddie Niedzwiecki was signed from Wrexham in the summer of 1983.

Back in the summer of 1979, there was a chance at last for the club and its fans to lick its wounds and prepare for the fight to regain our place back in the First Division. No easy task, as sides like West Ham and Sunderland were also highly fancied alongside us – as were Birmingham City, who had also suffered relegation.

On a personal note, I decided to leave the building trade to become a buyer at John Dickinson, who at the time were the biggest employers in Hemel Hempstead, with over 4,000 employees. It was a curious place, and being a paper mill it was strictly no smoking on site. If you broke that rule then it was instant dismissal, though I suspect that that rule was constantly being broken as there was often an aroma of cigarette smoke in the gents' toilets. Looking back, it was a great place to work, and after my initial fears as to whether I would take to office life and being a buyer it was indeed a bit of a doddle. Quite often me and my mates would grab some document that we thought looked important, and then casually walk around the huge site for a chat with not one person asking us what the hell we were doing. It was there where I first met the other members of what would make up the first band I was in, the Intros, where I would perform my own songs, which led me to believe that I must be doing something right as we were made up like so many other bands, as a collective of massive egos all vying for the spotlight. All in all, this change in my working life led me to finding friends I still have to this day.

During that summer, Vicky and I went our separate ways. In retrospect, I think she wanted me to settle down and to start taking responsibility for our future, whereas I on the other hand wanted to be a rock star, which would probably account for the split. Newly single, it was back out with my mates for the weekly round of pubs, football, badminton and golf. It was a situation that I found to be a bit of a shock as after having a girlfriend for the last few years, I was a bit lost among the visceral world of nights out with the lads. Suddenly I went from having a girlfriend who worried about me and my ever-changing moods to a reality that my mates couldn't give a toss if I was having one of my 'black dog' days as Sir Winston Churchill so aptly put it. Finally, I had to face the fact that I just had to get on with it.

In the August of that year, I went to the south of France with three other mates, presumably in the hope that we'd see the sights – scantily clad girls on the beach at Saint-Tropez. This holiday meant that I would miss Chelsea's opening three fixtures of 1979/80, against Sunderland at the Bridge, West Ham at Upton Park, and at home to Wrexham. We soon discovered that one of the worst things about France was the French. France is a nation that carries around a massive chip on its shoulder which means that however hard it might try, it must in the end come to the realisation that it will never be England. If that sounds jingoistic, so be it.

During our stay, which coincided with a French national holiday, we were routinely ignored by the locals who all seemed to possess the ability to spot an Englishman at 100 paces. So fed up was I with this situation that I decided to go on my own expedition across France and somewhat selfishly, left my mates to face the music – yet another example of the callousness of youth.

* * *

While I'd been in France, Chelsea had opened their campaign with a goalless home draw against Sunderland followed by a 1-0 victory at West Ham, thanks to Gary Johnson's early goal. Not a bad start, I thought, especially the win over the Hammers who were perhaps the favourites that year for promotion from the Second Division. What made that victory especially sweet was that one of my mates on that holiday, Mick, supported West Ham. It had been a long time since I'd held bragging rights over any of my friends concerning Chelsea's fortunes, so I made sure that I savoured every drop of the Blues' unexpected triumph at Upton Park to the nth degree.

On the morning I left the campsite in Saint-Tropez for the walk to Saint-Raphaël to catch the train, I'd already decided to take a detour and have a look at Marseilles, which had always had a reputation for being extremely sleazy and one of the biggest dens of iniquity in the whole of the European continent. Unsurprisingly, Marseilles didn't let me down. I felt a pervading sense of unease as there were nefarious, shady-looking customers standing on every street corner. By the time evening rolled around, I was fast going into a state of hysterical paranoia that someone was following me. Every time I looked back over my shoulder, I kept on noticing this rather unkempt, shabby excuse for a human being behind me. He looked as though he hadn't seen soap and water for at least a decade. He also had wild, staring eyes, set deep in his face which was adorned by a huge bushy beard. When I arrived at the railway station ready to move on to my next location, I thought I'd shaken him off. For safety's sake I took refuge on the platform next to the rest of the human flotsam that were commonly known as backpackers, to spend that night sleeping on the platform to catch the train for the next part of my odyssey, the French Alps.

In spite of the close proximity of my fellow travellers on that platform, I still wasn't in the mood to take any chances and actually slept with my Bowie knife under my bedroll. As the sun began to rise that morning I started collecting my stuff together ready to depart Marseilles; I was almost certain that I would never set foot in the place again. It was at that moment that I noticed the bearded nutter who'd been following me the previous day, was, to my horror, staring at me from the end of the platform, and yes, this time, there was no mistake, I was his person of interest. For fuck's sake, I thought – what is it with this bloke? Why is he so bloody fascinated with me?

When the train pulled in, I was one of the first to climb aboard to find myself a carriage so that I could get away from this disturbing situation. I then waited feverishly for the train to start moving for what seemed an eternity. So far, so good. No sign of the nutter on the platform. Suddenly I looked into the corridor of the train and there he was, staring into my compartment, and let me tell you, it was a bug-eyed stare. By now I'd lost all patience with this psycho and reached for my Bowie knife. Would I have used it? Most probably not but at least it would show him that I'd had enough of his bizarre behaviour. Thankfully, before I was forced to take any action, two gendarmes appeared from nowhere and grabbed him by the shoulders and he was frogmarched off the train. The madman still had the bloody nerve to look over his shoulder as he was being led away by the police, and once again, I was treated to the glare of those mad, staring eyes, looking at me, it has to be said, with unbridled hatred. At last the train pulled out of Marseilles and I was on my way to the French Alps. I would like to say that I've been to worse ratholes than Marseilles. I'd like to say that, but sadly, Marseilles is definitely a case of once seen, best forgotten.

It was while I was in the Alps that I made a new friend, Clive, who was, of all things, an officer cadet at Sandhurst. He was the embodiment of the quintessential Englishman abroad; not a hair out of place, clean-shaven, for God's sake he even wore a cravat whereas I looked like I'd been dragged through a hedge backwards. He once enquired of me if I would like to borrow his electric razor. 'Perhaps you'd like to have a shave, old chap?'

I replied, 'Nah, you're all right. I'm thinking of growing a beard,' which was a downright lie but seemed the politest comeback I could think of at the time.

In the end we both decided that we'd had enough of France and its natives and so decided to head for Paris where we'd stay overnight and then catch the train from the Gare du Nord and then on to Calais to catch the ferry back to dear old Blighty.

By the time we reached the French capital, we were both, in a word, broke. Our plan was to find a cheap hotel for the night and seek out a place where we could eat whatever our meagre funds would stretch to. We then had a stroke of good luck while on the metro. We got talking to a Scottish couple, Eileen and Sandy Shand. Somehow I managed to curb my desire to ask old Sandy if he was a relative of Jimmy Shand, a Scottish bandleader whose album celebrating Hogmanay was brought out every 365 days so that my family could celebrate the birth of a new year.

I have vivid memories of everyone in my family dancing around to the sound of the bagpipes, while I, being a miserable little git, sat down in an armchair sipping me and my sister's Christmas treat, Emva Cream Sherry. Not even the heady warm feeling from the alcohol could persuade me to leave the comfort of that chair. This is a trait I still carry to this day.

Fast forward to 1999 and I went to see the original cast of *Mamma Mia!*, the stage show, during the opening week. With everybody around me standing up, singing and dancing around to the medley of ABBA hits that signalled the end of the show, I sat resolutely down in my seat, arms folded. I was encouraged to get up and join in, but I wasn't having any of it. In my mind, I knew more about ABBA than the rest of these Johnny-come-latelys. I can clearly recall watching ABBA win the Eurovision Song Contest in 1974 in Brighton, with their song 'Waterloo', which became an instant hit. After that chart success, ABBA seemed to disappear leading to most people's opinion, that they were nothing more than just a one-hit wonder. That all changed in the autumn of 1975 when they released the epic 'SOS', a single that I rushed out to buy immediately after hearing it for the first time. Though I have to admit, that back then, ABBA were still considered a bit of a guilty pleasure. It was when I saw Elvis Costello and the Attractions performing a cover of 'Knowing Me, Knowing You' that I realised that if ABBA were good enough for Elvis, then consequently, they were good enough for me. The rest, as they say, is now history, and in my estimation, I would put ABBA just slightly behind the Beatles when it comes to the craft of creating the perfect pop song.

Back in Paris, Sandy and Eileen asked if we'd like to meet up with them that night to get something to eat. There was a bit of a silence before we came clean and admitted that unfortunately we were both a bit financially embarrassed.

'Never mind that, lads,' said Sandy. 'It'll be our treat.'

We agreed to meet later on after we'd found somewhere to stay, Eileen and Sandy in an upmarket hotel while me and Clive were left with no choice, owing to our lack of funds, than to spend that night in what can only be described as a flophouse.

During our meal that evening at some small, Parisian bar, I noticed that there were couples dancing on the postage stamp that passed for a dance floor. The next thing I knew was that Clive, forever the true English gent, asked Eileen if she wanted to dance. Eileen, I should point out, was in her mid-to-late 30s while Sandy was well into his 60s. Unlike today, when 60-year-olds still wear clothes that they wore in their 20s and 30s, I'm thinking stuff like Fred Perry, Harringtons, and the like – in those days, people really looked their age, Sandy being no exception. After Clive came back to the table, I thought, OK, now I'll have to ask Eileen for a dance, an offer she graciously accepted. Eileen, shall we say, was still an attractive woman. Suddenly, I found myself getting a bit too close to Eileen on the dance floor, a move she did nothing to discourage. Bloody hell, I thought, Sandy stands us both a meal and now I'm groping his wife right in front of him. I had a quick look over Eileen's shoulder but thankfully Sandy was engrossed in conversation with good old Clive. When our dance was over, we returned to the table. It seemed that I was in the clear as Sandy never said a word about the close proximity that I'd been enjoying with his wife. Clive, however, was more observant and quietly leaned over to me and had a word in my ear, 'Best not abuse our hosts' hospitality, old chap, don't you think?' In other words, stop groping this bloke's wife's arse. I had no answer. I'd been caught bang to rights.

'Yes, that would be best,' was my feeble reply, and thankfully the rest of the evening passed without a hint of indiscretion or embarrassment.

When I woke up the following morning in the fleapit that passed for our hotel, for some strange reason I decided to sniff my Converse basketball boots before putting them on. I'd been wearing them without socks for the past week in baking hot weather. The result of this stupidity was that one sniff of the aroma, which was repulsive to say the least, caused me to throw up in the sink. After I got over the waves of nausea, I joined Clive and then met Eileen and Sandy at the Gare du Nord for our trip back to Calais. Sandy and Eileen had first-class tickets for the train, of course, while me and Clive could only afford what was, in effect, one step up from steerage. Clive, however, was having none of it and insisted that we should join Eileen and Sandy in first class.

'But we haven't got a ticket,' I said.

'Don't worry about that,' was Clive's reply.

Sure enough, about halfway through our journey I saw a decidedly corpulent French ticket collector heading straight towards us. Shit, I thought. Now we're for it!

When the miserable-looking ticket collector asked for our tickets, Clive quickly took mine and handed it alongside his to the said collector, who I fully expected would explode into a torrent of Gallic fury. The collector shook his head, 'No,' and uttered sharply, in French, what must have been, in translation, that these are not first-class tickets, whereupon Clive berated the man in fluent French. It was the finest display that I've ever seen of steely British resolve. To my amazement, the collector then proceeded to bow and scrape his way past us while offering his apologies. To this day, not being conversant in French, I have no idea what Clive said, but, my God did he put that buffoon in his place. No wonder, I thought, that Sandhurst has the reputation as being the finest military academy in the world, if it was turning out blokes like that.

When we said our farewells at Victoria station, Sandy and Eileen headed to Euston to get the train back to

Scotland. For a few years, we actually sent Christmas cards to each other, but like so many acquaintances made at that stage of life they eventually disappeared into the ether, alongside Clive. After a bone-crunching handshake from Clive, he headed back to Surbiton, of course. I often wonder what happened to the three of them. I suppose Sandy is long gone, but what happened to Eileen? As for Clive, I worked out that he would have been just about the right age to be sent to the Falklands, three years later in 1982. God forbid that ever came to pass.

6

THIS BEING 25 August 1979, there was only one place that I was heading to, and that was Stamford Bridge to see Chelsea take on Wrexham. Though I'd travelled all the way across France, there was no way that I was going to miss the chance to go to my first game of the season. To think that I was allowed into the Bridge that day, still wearing my backpack, is something that would be inconceivable now due to the threat of suicide bombers, like the cowards who caused such devastation in London on 7 July 2005.

After our win at Upton Park on the Monday night against West Ham, there was a sense of optimism on the terraces where I stood in my favourite place of just in front of the tea bar – the same position that I'd been standing in since my first Blues game at the Bridge back in 1968. I got talking to some other lads who told me that we should have won on the opening day against Sunderland at the Bridge but somehow contrived to miss a glorious chance in the last minute when Micky Droy's header thumped against the foot of the post with Tommy Langley just failing to convert the rebound. This near miss would be the first of many that would come back to haunt us at the end of that season. I was also informed that we'd been battered at West Ham with the home side hitting the woodwork on numerous occasions. Yet Chelsea, who'd been completely outplayed, had scored from one of their two shots during the whole game to take all of the points.

There was a crowd of just over 18,000 there that day, on a gloriously sunny afternoon at the Bridge. Any sense of wellbeing I was feeling at being back in my spiritual home was shattered when Wrexham took an early lead. Bloody hell, I thought, here we go again. Thankfully, everyone's spirits were raised when Chelsea's equaliser arrived through the unlikely source of Ron Harris. As far as I can recall, I'd only ever seen Chopper score three goals. The first was up at the Baseball Ground against league champions Derby County in August 1972 when he hit a 20-yard piledriver into the roof of the net, our first goal in a brilliant 2-1 win. The second time I saw Chopper score was against Spurs at White Hart Lane when we came from behind to win 2-1 against the hated enemy.

That day against Wrexham, the game was still deadlocked at 1-1 with just a few minutes left. Oh, well, I thought, a draw is better than nothing. To be quite honest I was out on my feet after my exodus across the length and breadth of France. Then, with just two minutes to go, little Ian Britton gave the Blues the lead. Now Wrexham had to throw caution to the wind and as so often happens in football, they fell for the old one-two sucker-punch as John Bumstead added Chelsea's third, right on full time. Suddenly, my tiredness and exhaustion disappeared. It's amazing that seeing your team winning can give you such an adrenalin rush. When the final whistle blew, I thought we must be near the top of the league, which was a novelty in itself (in fact we were fifth).

I then made the weary journey back to Hemel Hempstead, whereupon my parents, rather than showing unbridled joy that their long-lost son had returned, asked, quite pointedly, I thought, 'What the hell are you doing back here?' As the saying goes, there is, after all, no place like home.

Playing for Wrexham that day were future Chelsea legends Eddie Niedzwiecki and the buccaneering full-back Joey Jones, who would both go on to be one of the reasons why the club roared back to the top flight five long years later. I think I'm right in saying that we made a couple of attempts at signing Jones before manager John Neal was finally successful in bringing the fiery Welshman to the Bridge. Young Mike Fillery made a good start to the season considering the pressure he was under as he was now recognised as the long-term replacement for the much-missed Ray Wilkins, who by now had sadly departed for Manchester United. Indeed, Fillery scored his first goals of the season in a 2-2 draw at Plymouth in the League Cup. Sadly there was to be no run in that competition that season as Chelsea construed in their own special way to lose the second leg at the Bridge to the unfancied Devon side. Even more disappointing were the two reverses in the league that this game against Plymouth was played between. A 2-1 defeat to Newcastle at St James' Park was followed a week later by a disappointing 2-1 home loss to Birmingham City.

There was an air of unease that day at the Bridge. The Blues now sat 11th in a division in which they were expected to be at least among the promotion contenders. That air of unrest must have seeped through to the boardroom as it was announced soon after that Chelsea would be parting company with manager Danny Blanchflower, who confirmed himself that he'd been thinking of quitting before the decision was made. Looking back now, it seems quite obvious that Blanchflower was a man out of time. He still upheld the old Corinthian spirit and values of a game that was becoming more cynical and cut-throat as the years went by. I can only imagine what Danny would have thought of football today where the craving for success has almost reached a level of insanity, such as the hiring and firing of managers just to keep the fans happy. That culture has pervaded not only among the top clubs, but lower-league sides, who have never come close in their history to any notable success. But that's the modern world, a time where patience has long since been considered not to be a virtue.

That game against Birmingham was also the last for Chelsea legend Peter Osgood. It was also the last appearance for a certain Trevor Aylott – though in no way could the latter's departure be met with as much sadness as the final sight of Ossie at the Bridge. Since Aylott's two winning goals on consecutive Saturdays back in 1977, he had fallen down the pecking order and was no more than a peripheral figure in regard to the first team. By the following Saturday, new manager Geoff Hurst was in place. Any hopes for an immediate improvement were dashed when Chelsea were humiliated 3-0 at Gay Meadow against Shrewsbury. It must have been a humbling experience for World Cup hero Hurst to witness that shambles. I, and many others of the Blues faithful, wondered when all of this nightmare would come to an end as Chelsea now occupied 18th place in the league, a position that was, quite frankly, unacceptable.

* * *

Another player who was axed by Hurst was Scottish international Eamonn Bannon, who'd only arrived at the Bridge back in January, when he was seen by Blanchflower as a useful addition to a midfield clearly lacking Wilkins's influence and leadership. The trouble was that by the time Bannon was signed, relegation was now becoming a reality. Bannon actually went on to have a successful career back in

Scotland with Dundee United and played a starring role in their run to the UEFA Cup Final a few years later.

It soon became apparent that Hurst did not share Blanchflower's opinion of Bannon as Mike Fillery, a talented and elegant midfielder, was always going to be his first choice. After a few seasons, Fillery decided that Chelsea no longer matched his ambitions and he moved on to QPR, of all clubs. It turned out that Fillery's decision to jump ship in the summer of 1983 was a disastrous one, as he barely made an impact during his time at Loftus Road, whereas Chelsea, at last, were on the cusp of an upturn in their fortunes.

The week after the debacle against Shrewsbury, Chelsea were due to face Watford at the Bridge and seeing that most of my mates supported the Hornets, I was worried sick that by five o'clock on the Saturday my life would not be worth living if the Hertfordshire club left with all the points. All week long I had put up with the jibes about how they were going to 'do' Chelsea. To be quite frank, I could see why they had so much confidence. Watford were in the middle of their rise from the Fourth Division to the top flight under the managership of Graham Taylor, and the deluge of cash that chairman Elton John was pouring into the club that he had supported as a boy. Thankfully my fears and trepidation were unfounded as the Blues ran out comfortable 2-0 winners with Watford looking strangely subdued that afternoon, Gary Johnson grabbing both goals.

The journey back to Hemel Hempstead was a mixture of relief and anticipation as I was due to go out to our regular Saturday-night haunt, the Wagon and Horses pub, which was right near the infamous funny roundabout. It was, in truth, a bit of a dive and had a reputation for trouble. I can remember that there always seemed to be a huge turnover of management. Indeed, I can recall one landlord who we christened Dr Light, being stabbed in the leg with a fork, while trying to placate a boozed-up Sunday diner who had complained that his roast was 'fucking cold!' Despite Dr Light's protestations that his staff would never serve up such a tawdry meal, these excuses counted for naught. Not surprisingly, he soon disappeared to make way for yet another poor sap of a landlord. Years later, the council decided that they wanted to be rid of this edifice and got their way when the poor old Wagon and Horses was demolished. It's strange that some boozers, no matter how many facelifts they go through, never manage to shake off that reputation of being trouble.

The main problem for the Wagon and Horses was that it was the chief destination for people who would later go on to Hemel Hempstead's ultimate nightspot, Scamps, or The Living Room, or any of the other many names that faceless dump went through. Blokes and girls alike used to take advantage of the lower prices in the Wagon and Horses before heading off to the disco where the prices for drinks were heavily inflated, despite their beer being as weak as the water that flowed through the River Gade which was situated at the back of the club. All it needed in that fevered atmosphere of boozed-up lads and tipsy girls was for some bloke to take too much interest in some other geezer's bird and then all hell would break loose.

That Saturday night at the Wagon and Horses, I found my Watford-supporting mates to be in a very subdued mood, with all of them acting as though their defeat at the Bridge that afternoon to the Blues was of no consequence whatsoever. No matter how hard I tried to bait them, there was no breaking their resolve that their club was going somewhere, a belief that bore fruit over the next five years. Following that victory over the Hornets, Chelsea went on their way to a five-game winning run that put us right among the front-runners for promotion. Excited by the turn of events, I talked my brother-in-law, Monty, into coming to the Bridge with me to see us roll over neighbours Fulham, which seemed very much to be on the cards, but as the Beatles so aptly put it, 'I Should've Known Better' as Chelsea, despite having the majority of possession, went down 2-0 to their local rivals on a sunny afternoon.

As me and Monty made our way back up Kings Road, I let my brother-in-law go ahead as he wanted to buy some new shoes. Like myself, Monty was very fashion-conscious. My abiding memory of that journey is of seeing him dart from side to side of Kings Road, which was and still is, one of the most fashionable places in the UK for the people who like to think that they are members of the in-crowd. Indeed, I can still recall walking past Vivienne Westwood and Malcolm McLaren's boutique which went under the name of 'Sex' at the time. I believe that later on it was called 'Seditionaries'. Of course, this was the birthplace of the Sex Pistols. I would like to say that I shopped there on many occasions, but sadly, even for those days, the clothes on display in their lurid shop window weren't exactly to my taste, being strictly a Harrington, Crombie, Doc Martens type of punter. Unfortunately, Monty never did find the shoes he was looking for despite his desperate search. So, with Monty being shoeless, and Chelsea being pointless, we decided that the only solution was the pub followed by a curry – the classic Saturday night institution.

I'd actually been invited to my mate's engagement party but the thought of attending was something that I was desperate to avoid. He had only met this girl in July that year and now in October, he was actually planning on spending the rest of his life with her. According to him, 'I just can't seem to get her out of my head.' Those proved to be empty words. Just two years later, rather than not being able to get this girl out of his head, he now seemed to be hell bent on getting her out of his life forever when he jilted her a week before they were due to go to the altar. His excuse, that some long-lost uncle had died during the week before the wedding, must go down as one of the most mind-numbing, lamest excuses I've ever heard. This mate of mine was not exactly free with money; in fact he was a right bleeding tight wad. So, unbelievably, he suggested to the jilted bride to be, 'Let's go on the honeymoon, anyway.' Incredibly she agreed but as the old saying goes, if you write 'welcome' on your forehead, then people will invariably treat you like a doormat.

After a few drinks we went for a curry on Kings Road. You'd expect that because of the locale the food would be of the highest order but to be blunt it was awful, perhaps one of the worst curries I had ever had. Naturally, we decided that there was no way that they were going to get a tip for their lousy performance. Incredibly, as we were leaving the restaurant, a waiter came up and asked us, 'What about a tip?' Quick as a flash, Monty snapped back, 'Lower your prices, or go out of business,' and with that we departed the scene, leaving the waiter standing there, open-mouthed.

7

FOLLOWING THE home defeat to Fulham, seven days later Chelsea lost 2-1 to Sunderland at Roker Park which meant that the winning run had suddenly come to a grinding halt. The week after that Chelsea were due to play Orient at Brisbane Road. Now, I was also due to pick up my guitar in south London that day, a Rickenbacker 330, an iconic guitar used by the likes of Pete Townshend, Paul Weller and Roger McGuinn of the Byrds. I'd been after one of these for years and had finally saved up enough money to get one. During the week I had a call from my mate Mick, who asked if I'd be interested in going to the Orient game as our mutual friend Les, an Orient season ticket holder, had a spare ticket going because his brother couldn't make the match. I didn't really fancy it. A fixture at Brisbane Road didn't exactly bring back happy memories as the Blues had always found it a difficult place to visit and seeing that I was eager to get my hands on my brand-new Rickenbacker, I passed on the ticket.

When I got back to Euston that evening, I bought a paper to see how Chelsea had got on. I'd found out earlier while in the guitar shop that we'd been leading 2-0 at half-time but seeing that we'd blown a two-goal lead against the same opponents back in the infamous FA Cup fifth-round defeat back in 1972, I was taking nothing for granted. In trepidation I feverishly scanned the results. To say that I was shocked when I saw the scoreline is an understatement. Bloody hell, I thought, and there it was in black and white: Orient 3 Chelsea 7. Poor old Les, I thought, having to sit through that as Chelsea demolished his beloved Orient. Still, there was one consolation for Les – at least he didn't have to sit next to me, gloating and celebrating.

I was due to meet up with Les and my other mates the following Saturday after the Charlton game at the Bridge. We used to meet at Lancaster Gate where we would have a few drinks in a pub before going on to a disco that we rather cruelly christened as 'grab-a-granny' night. As you can no doubt work out, political correctness and wokeness had not been invented back in 1979. I should imagine that Les wasn't looking forward to seeing me that evening. I fully expected him to keep out of my way before we headed off for that desperate night in a meeting place for the lost and lonely. In truth, I could hardly rub it into Les, as I hadn't even gone to the game, spurning a ticket for a new guitar. As it turned out, I didn't get a chance to wind up Les. As soon as he walked into the pub he fixed an evil stare in my direction and mouthed the words, 'Don't you dare.' He needn't have worried. Revelling in a victory over one of your mates' teams is a precarious practice that can often come back to bite you hard. Football, as we all know, can be a nebulous experience to say the least.

During the week, I'd been to see the Blues take on West Ham at the Bridge. It was a wet, miserable night that was made even more miserable when West Ham took the lead through the curly haired Pat Holland's opener for the anything-but-chirpy Cockneys. The Hammers' cheers were stifled in their throats, however, when Lee Frost equalised five minutes later to add to the hat-trick he'd scored against Orient the previous Saturday. And that's the way it stayed until the 75th minute when Mike Fillery's close-range effort put the Blues 2-1 ahead. Although West Ham threw everything at the home side in the remaining 15 minutes, we held firm and took both points which meant a double over West Ham and also a personal victory for me given my best mate Mick's support of the Hammers.

For some reason I stood in the middle of the Shed that night instead of my usual place in front of the tea bar. Five years later in 1984, I wish I'd made the same decision because the tea bar was one of the main places that the West Ham mob charged into, seeking revenge for the 3-0 drubbing they'd received at the Blues' hands that day.

After our 3-1 win against Charlton, I asked my mate Jon, a Preston North End fan, if he wanted to come with me to the Bridge to see them take on the Blues, and though he wasn't what you'd call a fervent supporter of his local team, he said he'd be up for it. Jon was a tough-looking former Merchant Navy rating who I'd met at John Dickinson after I'd taken over his job because he was moving over to another section. Jon often regaled me with stories about mass brawls in places like Murmansk with Russian merchant seamen. It made my forays abroad seem very insipid indeed, almost like that film, *Travels with my Aunt*. Jon had also left the band he was in, where he was their keyboard player, to join up with me. I'd played him some of my songs whereupon he quit his current band of close mates to jump ship, something I was completely unaware of until Jon informed me at work, 'I've quit the band.'

'Why?' I enquired.

'Because I'm joining up with you, lad.' Highly flattered, it was an offer I could hardly refuse.

Sadly, for Jon, Preston surrendered quite meekly and after Micky Droy put the Blues ahead, there seemed to be an air of inevitability that they would take the points.

This was confirmed when Ian Britton scored the second goal in a comfortable 2-0 victory. It seemed I was on a roll. Three victories in just a few weeks against teams my mates supported meant that I finally had something to shout about. Apart from a disappointing 1-0 reverse to Oldham, by and large, Chelsea looked set to be in the fight in the charge for promotion. Indeed, if we'd not conceded an 88th-minute Clive Allen equaliser for QPR at Loftus Road, we'd have been only one point behind leaders, Newcastle. Still, second in the league was fine by me seeing that we'd made such an indifferent start to the campaign. If only we'd known that QPR's equaliser in the 2-2 draw that night would be one of the reasons to why the season ended in a case of so near, yet so far.

* * *

The next home game would be a decisive one against Leicester who were also in the race for the top flight, a situation they had continuously found themselves in through the late 1970s and early '80s. Before that Boxing Day clash, I was due to sample for the first time a night out with my workmates at a top nightspot which at the time went by the name of Baileys, in Watford. All of the people on my buying section were going, plus a few more from other locations in the offices of John Dickinson. Unfortunately Jon, my new bandmate who'd been rather cruelly flirting for months with one of the middle-aged women on our section, now had to pay the price that evening for his callousness. To Jon, who was 23, this was all a bit of a lark but to the 46-year-old lady, who shall remain nameless, this was deadly serious. Jon had told her that he fancied women in tight pencil skirts and black stockings. I warned him that the said lady had a crush on him, and he just laughed it off, saying it was only a joke. On the night of our outing, this poor, misled lady, turned up – you guessed it – in a tight-fitting pencil skirt and what looked like black stockings. Jon looked sick.

'Fuck me,' he said. 'What am I going to do?'

'Suffer,' was my curt reply.

The act on that night at Baileys was *New Faces* winner Patti Boulaye, someone who I had no interest in seeing at the best of times. Still, I thought, who cares, I'll be drunk anyway. During Miss Boulaye's performance, she proceeded to leave the stage and come down into the audience. Our table was right at the front so the sight of her singing to various men at their tables filled me with horror. What to do if she headed towards where I was sitting? The thought of being picked out and serenaded filled me with a blood-curdling terror. The blokes – or should I say victims – she picked on suffered their embarrassment with a typically stoic British attitude. So although I was praying that she wouldn't head for our table, what could I do? It would hardly be good form for me to tell her, 'Why don't you fuck off,' would it? Thankfully, and to my relief, she duly passed by where we were sitting and descended on some other poor old sap who was forced to wear a fixed grin during his execrable moment in the spotlight.

After her set had finished, I could finally relax. I then noticed that Jon had departed from our table. I quickly put two and two together and realised that he must be with the middle-aged lady in question, from our office, who quite honestly believed that Jon's advances were more serious than he had intended. When he came back to the table he looked ashen-faced. He told me that when he'd informed her that it had all been just a bit of a laugh, she had burst into tears, and told him that he had no right to lead her on like that, and that consequently, for both of them, the thought of Monday morning and facing each other and their workmates was indeed, a very grim prospect.

My already eventful evening then took another surreal turn when my ex-girlfriend, Vicky, appeared on the stage with her new fiancé to announce their engagement along with some other anxious-looking couples. I felt a mixture of incredulity and horror, that someone I'd gone out with for a few years would submit themselves to this horrendous humiliation, as the master of ceremonies said, 'Let's have a big hand for our Christmas lovebirds!' I felt a sinking feeling in my stomach with the realisation that no matter how close you are to someone, what lies beneath in their psyche will, in reality, always be a mystery.

Was I shaken up by this? Yes, of course, but I quickly decided to have a few more drinks and then head on to the dance floor in search of female company. With some bizarre act of revenge on my mind, I spotted my assistant boss standing alone watching the dancers on what is one of the loneliest places in the world – the dance floor. She was 42 years old, but in a word, fit. So, I plucked up the courage to ask her for a dance which she thankfully accepted. When we were having our dance to some god-awful slushy ballad, I decided to chance my arm to make my move. To my surprise, my kiss was eagerly received. Then I saw Vicky dancing next to us with the goon who passed for her fiancé and the look on her face was a picture, one of utter horror that her ex-boyfriend was necking with an older woman who was married with two sons. I've always believed that revenge is a dish best served cold, and to my shame I found some joy at Vicky's reaction. It was only when the senior buyer collared me as I left the dance floor, remarking, 'Bloody hell! You dirty dog! What have you done?' Like a ton of bricks, it then hit me that on Monday morning I would be sitting opposite her at our respective desks. Suddenly, I felt stone-cold sober.

The journey back from Baileys in the minibus was, to be honest, bleak. Jon's spurned middle-aged lady was weeping alongside my assistant boss who was being comforted by some of the other women who were sympathising with her tears. Some of the looks that were directed towards me and Jon from our female workmates were downright evil and withering. I was incredibly relieved when I was dropped off with one of the young office girls for a long, cold walk home. We spoke of the events but somehow skirted round what I'd got up to. As we parted company, she suddenly asked me, 'What were you doing kissing that old bag?' a remark she seemed to think was hysterically funny. For once, I had no words and sheepishly walked off into the night.

For the next two days I had the worst case of the fear that I'd ever experienced. What the hell would I say to my kissing partner on Monday? When you're 24 years old, 42 seems a lifetime away and back in those days, the age gap was more defined than it is now when people over 40 act like they're still in their 20s, or in some cases, younger. Thankfully for me, nothing was ever mentioned between us, and for her silence and maturity in dealing with this embarrassment so discreetly, I will be forever grateful.

* * *

Back to football. Our opponents, Leicester City were just below us in the table. There was no doubt that this would be a tough game and on Boxing Day I stood there once again in front of the tea bar with that seasonal smell of cigar smoke, newly acquired aftershave, and even the faint aroma of whisky, which had no doubt been consumed in vast quantities the previous day in front of the telly. I always used to find those Boxing Day fixtures to have a rather muted atmosphere, most probably due to the fact that the majority of the crowd were still nursing terrible hangovers. The game was a tense affair with nothing to choose between the sides. That was until the 65th minute when Mike Fillery fired the Blues ahead. Manfully, Chelsea managed to see it out despite Leicester's best efforts and took the points with a 1-0 win.

Relieved and happy that we got the victory, I set out from the Bridge to meet up with my mates in the West End where we had tickets for the Leicester Square Odeon to see Disney's effort as they tried to cash in on the *Star Wars* craze that had exploded in the UK and the rest of the world during the last couple of years. Unfortunately, *The Black Hole* was execrable, and that's putting it mildly. After a massive publicity campaign, it was a box-office disaster that left Disney with an abject excuse of a film on their hands. Though, having said that, in a way it did live up to its title and quickly disappeared into a black hole never to be seen again.

Chelsea's next game over the holiday period looked the easiest on paper but as the saying goes, football isn't played on paper and inexplicably, the Blues went down 2-0 to Wrexham at the Racecourse Ground. Just three days later after our triumph over Leicester, the next away match against Luton at Kenilworth Road looked an even tougher prospect. Yet, once again, Chelsea displayed their ability to surprise their following by gaining a creditable 3-3 draw in an exciting see-saw fixture that saw them take an early lead, then go behind twice before Clive Walker levelled just 60 seconds after Luton had scored what they presumed was the winning goal. Still, not a bad start to the new decade, I thought.

Yet still, our consistency, which had been a continuous problem during the entire history of the club, was still rearing its ugly head on a decidedly regular basis. This trait was startlingly evident in the next three games, all at the Bridge, the first of which was against table-topping Newcastle. This was undoubtedly our biggest match of the season, a game that I took my new girlfriend, Valerie, to. I'd met her at Hemel's go-to nightclub, The Living Room, on New Year's Eve, and even though she had no interest in football even she could understand what she witnessed that day, beside me at the Bridge as Chelsea tore the Geordies apart 4-0, with winger Walker having one of his finest games in a blue shirt. On that performance, I, and many others in attendance that day, thought that promotion was now very much a possibility.

I was due back at the Bridge in 48 hours' time for the Monday night game against Wigan Athletic in the third round of the FA Cup, which had been delayed due to a mixture of the weather and the fact that Wigan's previous tie had gone to a replay. On a bitterly cold night that reduced the playing surface to an ice rink, the Latics took full advantage of the treacherous conditions which proved to be a leveller that Chelsea just couldn't deal with, allowing the visitors to come away with a shock 1-0 victory. It was a classic example of 'after the Lord Mayor's Show' following the sparkling performance against Newcastle. Here we were just two days later, being dumped out of the cup at home by a Third Division side. I doubt in today's day and age that this game would even have taken place. The pitch, to all intents and purposes, was dangerous. All the fleet-footed skills of players like Mike Fillery and Clive Walker were negated on that bone-hard surface as the Latics came away that night with a famous, if not wholly deserved, victory.

The Lancashire side were once again the visitors at the Bridge in the third round of the FA Cup in January 1985. Once again, the pitch was frozen solid and so the skills of

Pat Nevin, Kerry Dixon and David Speedie were hampered against their less-talented opponents. I can recall standing there, chilled to the bone, watching Wigan take a two-goal lead by half-time. I heard later that my girlfriend's sister's Luton supporting boyfriend was dancing round the front room when he saw the score. I hope he enjoyed himself because in the second half the Blues fought back with Pat Nevin scoring the equaliser from an overhead kick. Even my joy at the ball hitting the back of the net was curtailed when, owing to the freezing cold weather, I put my back out of place and faced the long trek home to Hemel Hempstead in agony. Still, at least we were still in the cup, if only just, as the game ended 2-2. With the tricky prospect of a replay to face at Springfield Park, our trepidation was proved groundless when the replay took place a few weeks later. By this time the game was played on a pitch that was at least playable. Chelsea fully exploited the gap in class by wiping the floor with Wigan, winning 5-0 with Dixon hitting four of the goals.

Back in January 1980 I dreaded going into work the following day, fully expecting the ribbing I was going to have to face. Someone thought it would be hysterical to leave a piece of paper on my desk with the scoreline written on it. How clever, I thought. Laugh? I thought I'd never start.

Our next home fixture was against Shrewsbury, who'd battered us back in September in Geoff Hurst's first game in charge of the Blues. Surely this was a prime opportunity to mete out some form of revenge for the drubbing we'd received at Gay Meadow. Well, unfortunately not, as Chelsea miserably capitulated 4-2 in one of the worst Bridge performances that season. After Tommy Langley had equalised Shrewsbury's early opener, the Blues then contrived to concede two goals in two minutes to be 3-1 down at the break. Any hope of a comeback was terminated when Shrewsbury added a fourth a few minutes from time. And even though Langley added his second of the afternoon, it was all too little, too late. These aberrations were starting to become a habit, one we had to break if we had any ambitions to get back to English football's top table.

I'll be honest, I believed then and even more so now in retrospect, that if we'd gone up in 1980 then it was almost certain that it would be a carbon copy of the previous season when we had been the First Division's whipping boys. On the other hand, what true fan would be satisfied with just plodding along in their various leagues, year in, year out? You want to believe that your club has ambitions to succeed that matches the hopes and dreams of the faithful who turn out in their thousands every Saturday. Was this current Chelsea side as good as the 1976/77 promotion winners? I don't believe so. This team definitely lacked someone of the stature of Ray Wilkins and though Hurst was doing a decent job so far, he didn't exactly inspire the drive and determination that Eddie McCreadie had imbued in the fine young side he'd created.

The main problem was that just like back in 1977, the club was still broke, which was the reason we'd only lasted for two years back in the top flight. With funds still scarce, in my estimation the same depressing outcome that we'd previously experienced would surely have become inevitable. The thought of being what is known today as a yo-yo club was a bleak prospect. The epitome of this title has to be Norwich City who have proved to be too good for the Championship, yet sadly lacking when it comes to life in the Premier League.

* * *

The following Saturday, Chelsea would make the short trip to play Watford at Vicarage Road, a game I would go to with a couple of my mates who both supported the Hornets. I used to dread these matches against our local team as my life would be made hell for a couple of weeks after if the Blues somehow came up short. When we parked the car on that cold, windy day back in February 1980, it was evident that Chelsea were in town as the blue and white hordes had pervaded every corner of the area, leaving the locals looking nervous and doing their best to avoid the visitors' crew as they menacingly made their way to the ground.

I've seen on a website called Goodreads that one of my previous books was marked down to two stars because the reviewer thought there was an air of zeal in my writing regarding the hooliganism that was endemic back in the 1970s and '80s. It's true, Chelsea did have a reputation for trouble, and though sometimes it got out of hand, and was indeed very ugly, I can't lie and say there wasn't something visceral and exciting about going to games back in the day. I, and thousands of other young men who followed the club in those days, found a certain amount of pride in the fact that the Blues had a hard reputation when it came to mixing it with rival fans.

Perversely, our support grew even more passionate when the club fell on hard times; a sense of blind devotion was evoked that the further Chelsea's fortunes plummeted, the more fervent the support became, which is why I find today's attitude of the Johnny-come-latelys a very bitter pill to swallow, especially the young fans who spew venom of utter vitriol on sites like Twitter every time a result goes against the Blues. I wonder how many of them would cope with what we had to put up with in those days? You see, when I first supported Chelsea, they were a glamorous side, packed with stars and had an elan and style that set them apart from most other teams. Manchester United, with George Best, Denis Law and Bobby Charlton, were the only other team that could match the star quality that was on offer back at the Bridge in those days. Then of course, there were the trophies, when during consecutive seasons we'd won the FA Cup and the European Cup Winners' Cup. To see all of that disappear in just a few short seasons was extremely hard to take. How many, I wonder, would stick with the club if they were to ever fall on hard times again? Not many, I suspect, not with the current trend being the need and desire for instant success, something that has become an insane prerequisite these days.

As so often was the case when Chelsea were in town, they always made sure that their opponents had their biggest crowd of the season. Though the Blues were commonly known as a sleeping giant, their scalp was still prized among the other teams in the Second Division. The game at Vicarage Road was more like a cup tie with Watford's direct, route-one approach a polar opposite to Chelsea's more considered, stylish way of playing. That's not to say that Watford's tactics weren't effective. Back in those days I hated playing against teams that adopted this tough, physical style. Though they had a skilful winger in future England international John Barnes, with Nigel Callaghan on the other flank, the majority of the Hornets' side looked like they were extras from the TV show *Land of the Giants*. Although Watford huffed and puffed, Chelsea were leading 2-0 at the break with Gary Johnson's goal putting the Blues completely in the driving seat with just a minute remaining of the first half.

We all knew what to expect in the second period – an all-out aerial onslaught from the home side. Chelsea were dropping deeper and deeper and sure enough, midway through the second half, Watford pulled the inevitable goal back. The silent, passive, home crowd at last showed some signs of life and started to get behind their team. Though in fairness, I have to say that the blue and white of Chelsea's support was evident on all four sides of the ground.

As Watford poured forward they left themselves open to the counter-attack, a tactic that proved successful when Clive Walker restored the two-goal advantage with just a few minutes left. At 3-1 the game looked dead and buried but let's remember, we're talking about Chelsea, who have always had a history of snatching defeat from the jaws of victory. Any such belief was dispelled when Luther Blissett instantly put the home side back in contention. And though the precious seconds ebbed away at a witheringly slow pace, there was an air of inevitability when Watford were awarded a penalty in injury time. I was sick to the stomach. Only Chelsea could blow a 3-1 lead with just a few minutes remaining on the clock. Along with thousands of other Blues fans, I stood there in dumbfounded disbelief as Watford's Ian Bolton stepped up to take the spot kick.

One of my Watford-supporting mates remarked to me, 'There's going to be a bloody riot if he scores,' and seeing that the massive Blues following had already created havoc in the town centre, smashing in a few shop windows, I was inclined to agree with him. I could hardly bear to watch as Bolton hit his drive wide of the goal. Total despair was replaced by unbridled joy, in a split second. There was barely time to restart the game before the referee blew the final whistle. The sense of relief was tremendous. In fact, my legs were shaking, and I'd only been watching the game. I felt emotionally drained. My mates who followed the Hornets said they'd almost felt relieved when Watford missed that penalty, an attitude I found difficult to understand. But then again, I could see their point. Chelsea's reputation preceded them in those days. Back in 1975 when I went to see the

Blues at Kenilworth Road to take on Luton, our following had actually set a train on fire. So, in retrospect, perhaps my mates' trepidation at what would ensue had Watford equalised was, when all was said and done, justified.

I'd just like to say that I don't really look back with any affection at some of the incidents from that era, but it happened, and that's the way it was. There's no good sugar-coating it. When you went to a game then, you had to have your wits about you as trouble could be lurking at any time just around the corner. I'm not saying that I miss those days and the culture of violence, but somehow the modern experience of attending a Blues game, excluding the Mathew Harding Stand, is akin to being in a crowd that wouldn't be out of place in a West End theatre. There's no doubt that football, because of the increase in prices, has almost become a middle-class game. Suddenly the working class have been priced out of following our national sport when they were once considered to be the lifeblood.

So, after that victory over Watford, you'd have expected Chelsea to see off Cambridge United at the Bridge the following Saturday as the men from the Abbey Stadium were having a season that could be described, at best, as mediocre. Once again, my brother-in-law Monty came along as another shopping trip was planned. This time our destination would be Carnaby Street, where I was after a polka-dot skinny tie among other Mod apparel. The game was flat and uninspiring and after Cambridge had equalised Chelsea's early opener, it died and faded away into 90 minutes of extreme tedium and ended up in a tame 1-1 draw. Another point dropped was a bitter disappointment after the heroics at Vicarage Road the previous Saturday. Though we remained in a good position for promotion, Birmingham City, among others, were starting to close the gap. More slip-ups like this and we'd be in a situation of looking over our shoulder with a growing concern.

Still, our trip to Carnaby Street was successful as I found that polka-dot tie as well as a pair of penny loafers, and a button-down, checked Ben Sherman shirt, long-sleeved of course, which has always been my preference.

* * *

The Blues' next game was away at Bristol Rovers and would see the debut of new signing Dennis Rofe, who had just arrived from Leicester City for £80,000, a move which came as a bit of a shock as Leicester were right in the mix alongside us. Before that trip to Eastville, however, after feeling unwell for a couple of weeks with a persistent hacking cough, I came down with scarlatina, a milder form of scarlet fever. If I'd contracted the milder one, I'm so thankful that I never caught the more virulent version as the next month became a bit of a blur.

Scarlatina is a particularly nasty complaint. Apart from being covered in angry red spots from head to foot, you feel fatigued, have a terrible cough, and most worryingly find it hard to get a breath. Coming down with this meant that I was highly contagious and had to have my own cutlery, towels, etc. It also kept me housebound for a month. Normally, at the age of 24, that would be a nightmare but, going out was the last thing on my mind. In fact, on one Thursday night while trying to watch *Top of the Pops* – yes, I know, but old habits die hard – I really started to struggle to get a full breath, which is consequently a self-fulfilling prophecy, as the more you panic the more you can't breathe. Ergo, your breathing becomes even more panic-stricken. Not one to miss an opportunity for a bit of drama, I announced to my mum and dad, 'Get a doctor! I'm dying!'

Unlike today, when going to see a GP is an achievement in itself, my parents somehow managed to get an emergency doctor to come out and see me within half an hour. The first thing he did after assuring me that I wasn't dying was to inform me that I was suffering a panic attack. In those days, doctors were not averse to administering something that would calm you down, be it tablets like valium, mogadon, and various other tranquillisers, or as the Stones so aptly called them, 'Mother's Little Helper'. After consulting with my parents in our dining room, he asked me if I'd be OK with having an injection as a sedative to calm me down. 'Yeah, do what you've got to do,' was my weak reply.

I could see the relief in their faces as they were most probably worn out by my display of uninhibited hysteria at the thought of my early demise. I've got to say, whatever was in that injection did the trick. Within seconds I was feeling a wave of tranquillity and a sense of wellbeing I'd never experienced before.

Being confined to staying in, I lost touch with my mates, social life and the band which had grown from Jon and myself into a five-piece. If truth be told, some of the Blues' results also passed me by.

After a calamitous 3-0 defeat at Eastville, Chelsea then went on to win their next two games including a fine 2-1 victory over Fulham at Craven Cottage with a brace from the enigmatic Clive Walker, exacting full revenge for our defeat to them back in October. That win put us back to the top of the league. Things were looking good.

A midweek visit to St Andrew's to play Birmingham City was a tough prospect but after those two victories on the spin, I was hopeful that we'd come away with at least a point that night. I know you can't put it down to one game that defines your season, the argument being that so many factors decide upon where you finish up in the table, but the cold, hard facts are that if we'd lost to Birmingham by a narrower margin than the 5-1 thumping we received, Chelsea would have been promoted that year instead of the team from the country's second city.

During this time, Chelsea had signed Colin Lee for £200,000 from Spurs of all clubs. Lee had made a brilliant start to his career at White Hart Lane, scoring five goals on his debut against Bristol Rovers in a 9-0 win. Since then, however, he'd fallen from grace, becoming a peripheral figure. In retrospect, his decision to move across London to the Bridge was a wise one as before too long, Garth Crooks and Steve Archibald would arrive at Spurs which no doubt would have pushed Lee further down the pecking order as they were to be the first choice for the despised enemy over the next five years. Lee's arrival at the Bridge consequently led to Tommy Langley being marginalised as it was obvious that Geoff Hurst saw Lee as his main striker.

This was confirmed that summer when Langley was moved on to local rivals Queens Park Rangers for £400,000, a move that ultimately never really worked out for Langley, though he did come back to haunt the Blues, scoring twice against us the following season. Yet there is no doubt that Chelsea is Tommy Langley's spiritual home as he is now a season ticket holder at the Bridge, and was a regular on the now-defunct Chelsea TV, which I, for one, sadly miss.

8

BACK IN 1980, Chelsea's response was positive following that setback against Birmingham when they won their next three games, with Tommy Langley once more being given a run in the side as Geoff Hurst's new signing, Colin Lee, had picked up an injury and would spend the next few weeks out of the picture. After a vital 2-1 victory over Charlton at The Valley, thanks to Langley's 82nd-minute winner, Chelsea found themselves once more at the summit of the league. The only trouble was that our results were being matched by both Birmingham and Sunderland and more worryingly, even bettered when the Blues dropped points.

When I came away from The Valley on 29 March 1980, I quickly worked out that if we could win our next two home games against QPR and Luton, and get something from our difficult trip to Filbert Street to face Leicester City, then we would be in the driving seat for promotion. On the following Wednesday I went with my boss, who supported QPR, to the Bridge praying that we would overcome our west London rivals who had very little chance of breaking into the chasing pack. Perhaps that was the reason why Rangers played so well that night as they had no pressure or expectation on their shoulders, unlike the Blues who looked edgy and nervous. After QPR took the lead midway through the second half, my worst fears looked like they would be realised. As much as Chelsea threw everything at the visitors, it was perhaps almost inevitable that QPR would add to their lead. With just a few minutes left they doubled their advantage and a hammer blow had been dealt to Chelsea's hopes of a quick return to the top flight.

Not only did I have to put up with my boss gloating on the journey home, and believe me that was bad enough, but the prospect of facing him at work the following day was grim. Him being my superior, I could hardly tell him to 'wipe that fucking grin off your stupid face', could I? No, there was no way out. Yet again a Blues defeat at the hands of a team that someone I worked or socialised with meant that I'd just have to take my medicine – and take it like a man.

Away from football, now that I'd got over my illness, I was back rehearsing with my new band, the Intros; we were, to all intents and purposes, trying to be Elvis Costello and the Attractions. Since seeing Costello and the Attractions at the Hemel Pavilion in April 1978, I had become, not to put it lightly, obsessed with Costello's idiosyncratic songwriting and the raw power of his backing band, who in my opinion left the likes of the Jam, and other peers, in their wake. Don't get me wrong, I was a big fan of Paul Weller and co, and they produced some of the finest singles during that era, but as powerful a live act as they were, when it came to a depth of songwriting and a totally visceral assault on your senses, Elvis Costello and the Attractions are, to my mind, one of the finest bands this country has ever produced. So, in my songwriting and the band's playing, we were giving ourselves pretty big shoes to fill. As the writer in the band, I'd been obsessed with the Beatles, the Who, and the Kinks while growing up, and this was reflected in the songs I was coming up with. A noble enterprise, you might think, but even in the spring of 1980 the sand beneath the feet of new wave, and pop-rock bands, was already shifting. It became startlingly obvious that the explosion of punk and new wave, which first emerged in 1976, was fast becoming marginalised. Indeed, as early as the summer of 1978, the dreaded disco epidemic was already sweeping away everything that stood in its path.

And yet although I hugely admire the Bee Gees, who have written some brilliant songs, I still find it hard to forgive them for the aberration that was *Saturday Night Fever*, a film I'm glad to say I've never seen the whole way through. Yet I'm ashamed to admit that in late 1978 when I was going with my mates to see the Kinks at Reading University, we found ourselves with nothing to do in the afternoon and seeing that it was freezing cold, we decided to seek out the nearest cinema where we could at least be warm for a couple of hours. Unfortunately, the only film showing at the local fleapit was, to our horror, *Grease*, which had already spawned two massive hits in 'Summer Nights' and 'You're the One That I Want'. What a choice! Freeze to death all afternoon or watch a steaming pile of the brown stuff that would have you believe that John Travolta and Olivia Newton-John were actually teenagers. Really, this was the definition of Hobson's choice. Finally, we decided to swallow our pride and go into the cinema to watch what we considered to be populist drivel for the plebs. When we went to the box office to purchase our tickets, we were met by a bored-looking cashier who seemed to take immense pleasure in informing us, 'Sorry. We're full up.'

I felt like I'd been slapped in the face. To be turned away from a film I wouldn't have dreamed of seeing if I hadn't been so bloody cold was the epitome of humiliation. When we got outside, me and my mates resorted to blaming each other for this fiasco with accusations being thrown around like, 'It was your bloody idea in the first place!'

Thankfully, things got better that night as the Kinks were absolutely brilliant. What made it even better was that we met someone at the gig who had managed to get hold of the stamp that was used on your hand to say that you'd bought a ticket. So, after the embarrassment we had suffered that afternoon at the cinema, getting to see the Kinks for nothing was a good end to what had so far been a troubling day.

The following morning, before we set out on the journey back home from Reading, we swore an oath that none of us would ever let on what had happened at being turned away from watching *Grease*. However, now that four decades have passed, I feel comfortable coming clean at last.

* * *

In the music scene of the early 1980s, it was becoming increasingly obvious that guitar bands were fast disappearing when it came to the charts. What a time, I thought, to be involved in what was essentially a power-pop group with new wave sensibilities. Sadly the guitar, which had been king since rock music came along in the mid-1950s, was now in danger of being enveloped by the dreaded synthesiser, an instrument that I loathe to this day. If that wasn't bad enough, the emergence of the drum machine, especially the Syndrum, which would become endemic during that time, was horrific. Suddenly the charts were full of floppy-haired automatons, playing their synthesisers in A-frame setups. I hated every minute of bands like Depeche Mode, who sounded to me like they were using a Bontempi organ to a backbeat of a drum machine that sounded like a biscuit tin being beaten to death.

Things got even worse in the autumn of 1980 when the new romantics emerged – a collection of sad Bowie wannabes who somehow managed to take the worst excesses of the glam-rock era into their own perverted sense of what they laughingly imagined was style. Suddenly the charts were full of frilly-shirted mannequins with stupid haircuts. The main culprits were Spandau Ballet and Duran Duran, especially the latter whose flyblown posturing was made even more ludicrous by the singing ability, or lack of, of Simon Le Bon, who had a vocal range of about half an octave. How they got away with basically singing the same song, over and over again, with the only change being in the lyrics, beats me, the prime example being the dirge-like 'Save a Prayer' which is basically their go-to melody (if you can call it that) slowed down.

Then you had Spandau Ballet who treated us to the sight of men in kilts, posing while singing total rubbish, like the execrable 'Muscle Bound'. Then there was the sorry case of Visage with their banal offering, 'Fade to Grey', sung by the ludicrous Steve Strange, who always put me in mind of a navvy on a building site wearing makeup.

During that god-awful time, we also saw the rise of a certain Phil Collins, who'd previously been the drummer in Genesis, another band I loathed. At one time Peter Gabriel had been the lead vocalist. After he had quit the band, Collins was the unlikely choice to replace him as their frontman. Unfortunately, Collins was already losing his hair and had a face that looked like a bank robber who had a stocking pulled over his head. Amazingly, he went on to have a hugely successful solo career where he proceeded to release some of the blandest coffee-table pap I've ever had the misfortune to listen to.

Having said all of this, today's music scene almost makes the 1980s seem like a golden era.

Now we have to endure lightweight fluffy songs, sung by faceless wimps, bleating on about their sad, wasted lives. Yes, Ed Sheeran, I'm talking about you.

* * *

On the Saturday following the midweek defeat to QPR, Chelsea again fell short when they went down 1-0 to Leicester at Filbert Street thanks to Larry May's hotly disputed goal. The run-in that all of the Chelsea faithful were considering as just a mere formality a few weeks earlier was now becoming more problematic. Personally, I had a horrible feeling that out of the four teams in the race, Leicester, Birmingham, Sunderland and ourselves, we would be the ones to miss out on those precious top-three places. Losing to Leicester meant the game against Luton at the Bridge on the Monday had become a must-win. A crowd of nearly 30,000 were there and the atmosphere was, not to put too fine a point on it, unbearably tense. That anxiety seeped on to the pitch as once again the Blues looked jittery, a state of mind that Luton took full advantage of when Tony Grealish put the visitors ahead in the 24th minute. Where I was standing in front of the tea bar, and indeed all around Stamford Bridge, there was a deathly silence – that was apart from Luton's vast away following who had come to the game on a tandem. It was a sickening sight seeing their minuscule support on the North End terrace celebrating wildly.

Throughout the second half, not unsurprisingly, Chelsea absolutely battered Luton but just couldn't find that precious equaliser. All of our efforts seemed to be in vain until the 90th minute when recent signing Colin Lee scored his first goal for the Blues. Though it was celebrated with great joy and relief, it had come too late and a few minutes later the referee blew the whistle for full time. The feeling of elation at Lee's late strike was tempered instantly by the fact that yet again we had dropped another crucial point in a game that, truthfully, we should have won. One solitary point from our last three games was simply not good enough, and finally confirmed that Chelsea were now involved in a fight that would go all the way to the wire.

Another vital point was dropped the following week against Preston North End at Deepdale. After the home side had led by the only goal at half-time, Mike Fillery equalised nine minutes after the restart. Unfortunately, that was not enough to inspire Chelsea to go on to take the two valuable points that were up for grabs. The three teams around us carried on nicking crucial wins while Chelsea almost seemed to be the architects of their own downfall. Of all the times to hit an inconsistent streak of form the Blues, who had been culpable so many times, now looked to have every chance of once again shooting themselves in the foot. The stark reality for 1979/80, was that Chelsea's record against their three major rivals produced only one win. Birmingham had actually done the double over Hurst's team; two defeats that were to have disastrous ramifications for the club.

There's no doubt that being a supporter of a team is almost tougher than being one of the players. At least they are the masters of their own destiny while the fans are totally helpless, which I'm convinced creates a vicious circle of self-doubt that creeps into the team when things don't go well. This insidiously spreads to those on the terraces who then display their anxiety and stress straight back to the players wearing the blue shirts. The resulting state of mind is that everyone connected to the club is imbued with an impending sense of disaster. Though Chelsea managed to overcome Notts County the following week at the Bridge with Gary Chivers netting the only goal, this was followed seven days later with another 1-1 draw against Swansea at the Vetch Field. Yet again we'd thrown away a one-goal lead when the home side cancelled out Tommy Langley's first-half strike. The sad reality was that for the first time in months, Chelsea had somehow contrived to slip out of the top three.

The last time we'd been out of the promotion places was back in February following the home collapse against Shrewsbury. It's a stark reality to realise that those two games against the Shropshire side had ended in a 7-2 margin in their favour, a reality that was hard to stomach, and one that I would never have imagined happening when I first attended the Bridge back in 1968. Now our destiny was most definitely out of our hands.

* * *

The following Saturday, 3 May 1980, we had our last home game of the campaign at the Bridge against Oldham Athletic, which would also see the last appearance of the legendary Ron 'Chopper' Harris, whose career had spread over two decades and more than 700 games for his beloved club. Make no mistake, we shall never see his like again. Though, in fairness, John Terry pushed him quite hard when it came to total loyalty and the ethics of Chelsea Football Club. Sadly I suspect he will be the last in that line as players these days, like Romelu Lukaku, who kissed the badge upon his return to the Bridge, would most probably have preferred kissing the fat pay cheque he would be earning during his ultimately disastrous second spell with the club.

Any nerves that day against Oldham were dispelled when Fillery gave the Blues a sixth-minute lead. Clive Walker then went on to add two further goals and that's how the game finished – a comfortable home win to round off the season. Some poor misguided fools, mainly youngsters, invaded the pitch at the end, believing now that we had regained our position in the promotion places and that a celebration was in order. To my amazement some of the players even appeared in the directors' box to take a bow. Hang on a minute, I thought, aren't we jumping the gun here? Leicester had already been crowned champions that day after a 1-0 victory against Orient at Brisbane Road, while Birmingham had been made to sweat after only drawing 3-3 with Notts County at St Andrew's. Indeed, the home side had blown a two-goal lead that day and were then pegged back again after leading 3-2. Unfortunately for Chelsea, Notts County were unable to get that vital fourth goal which would have seen us promoted automatically.

So now the precarious situation became clear. Birmingham, who had finished on the same number of points as Chelsea with 53, but with a superior goal difference, would now have the long wait along with the Blues to see how Sunderland got on. Sunderland, who had drawn 1-1 at Cardiff City, were on 52 points but crucially still had a game in hand. A victory for Sunderland at home to West Ham would see them leapfrog both Birmingham and Chelsea into second place behind Leicester. The glaring truth was that Chelsea were now in prime position to become the fall guys.

FA Cup finalists West Ham were due to face Arsenal at Wembley just 48 hours before their visit to Roker Park. It didn't take much imagination to work out that their game against Sunderland would be no more than an afterthought, something to get through before they headed off to the beach that summer. Even if the Hammers had been beaten by the Gunners, as many people expected, how on earth would they regroup in such a short space of time after a Wembley defeat? For nine long days, once more every true Chelsea fan would suffer the agony of days when somehow, we hoped and prayed, somehow, just somehow, the Hammers would do us a favour, followed by days when in our heart of hearts we sadly knew that the game was up. It was a horrible feeling during that week, a feeling I can still recall.

On Saturday, 10 May West Ham upset the odds by beating hot favourites Arsenal 1-0 to win the FA Cup, thanks to Trevor Brooking's diving header. Following this unexpected triumph, it was pretty obvious that the Hammers would be celebrating lifting the cup. Well, you could hardly blame them. And sure enough, on the back page of the Sunday papers, alongside the match reports, there were also photographs of the players looking slightly worse for wear, celebrating at their banquet held after the game. I should imagine that it would have been very hard to find one sober member of West Ham's victorious squad that following morning, and the feeling must have been rife among all of their players that the Sunderland game was nothing more than an intrusion into what was a good old East End knees-up.

The Hammers' visit to Roker Park was almost akin to the way you felt at school on the last day before the summer holidays – let's just get this over with and then we can really start to enjoy ourselves. That Monday at work just dragged as the hours and minutes ticked by. I'd already resigned myself to my fate. The plan for that evening was to listen to updates on the radio in my music room, armed with a bottle of J&B whisky and a couple of joints. I had a nasty feeling that I'd be in need of both of them before the day was done. The memories of that lonely night are unsurprisingly hazy to say the least. The mixture of alcohol and weed combined dulled the pain as Sunderland inevitably grabbed the two vital points that saw them finish as runners-up and condemned Chelsea to another season in the Second Division, finishing in fourth place.

As a result of Chelsea's failure to win promotion, I was fully aware of what the following morning would bring. That moment of waking, still half asleep, when suddenly it hits you that your dream-like state is over and the harsh reality of what happened the previous night crashes down on you like a ton of bricks. According to reports in the morning papers, West Ham put up a decent display but with 48,000 Sunderland fans fervently willing their home team on, the club from Roker ran out comfortable 2-0 winners.

You might think that from that day on I bore a grudge against West Ham. Well, you'd be wrong. Although they hold no special place in my heart, there was only one reason why the Blues failed to regain their place in the top flight – their inability to turn frustrating draws into wins. Too many times we had failed to put teams away after dominating possession. Also, as I've previously mentioned, our record against the other promotion candidates was abysmal, and again I come back to the fact that though you can't point your finger at one game, as there were a myriad of reasons as to why the Blues came up short, that 5-1 defeat to Birmingham at St Andrew's was of huge significance as they took the previous third place on goal difference. If the three-points-for-a-win rule which came in at the start of the 1981/82 season had been in place a couple of years earlier, then Chelsea would have been promoted in 1979/80. Yet, as they say, 'if' is a little word with a big meaning. The grim truth was staring us in the face. Chelsea were still a Second Division club and I and many other Blues fans had a horrible nagging feeling that this situation was likely to stay around for the foreseeable future.

9

OVER THE next few years, the lack of ambition shown by the directors of the club had spread to the terraces. I personally fell into the trap of thinking that Chelsea were nothing more than an average Second Division side. Those glory days of the early 1970s were now definitely a thing of the past. During those times, it was hard to equate the current Chelsea side with the likes of Ossie and co. It was apparent that the club needed a new broom to come in and shake this crumbling edifice of a club out of its malodorous stupor, and to once again become a force in English football. That messiah was none other than Ken Bates, who bought the club for £1 in the spring of 1982. Bates is to this day a controversial figure among the Chelsea faithful, but in my opinion he saved the club from going out of existence when he fought the property developers who wanted to turn the Bridge into luxury flats. It's my firm belief that without his intervention there would now be no Chelsea Football Club. But more of him later.

In June 1980, me and Valerie, my on/off girlfriend, parted company. To be blunt, I just didn't feel that spark. No matter how hard I tried, there was something missing. The trouble was that she still wanted to carry on, and being a coward like most blokes, I let it drag far beyond its sell-by date before I finally had the guts to call it a day.

I know Woody Allen said, 'Sex without love is an empty experience, but as empty experiences go, it's right up there.' While that is brilliantly witty, in the nebulous experience of relationships, for me it doesn't hold water. Some blokes could string a girl along even though they could see no future with them. I was not one of their number. If the feeling isn't mutual, you're not only lying to your partner but you're lying to yourself.

Meanwhile, on the band front, things were going well. We were rehearsing hard and were ready to record our first demo. To say the results of our first visit to a studio were mixed is a gross understatement. In those days I was the lead singer in the band. The weekend before, I'd been camping in the Lake District which is famous not only for being a beauty spot but also vulnerable to wet and windy weather which is perhaps the reason for my going down with a heavy cold and a sore throat. Still, the show must go on, I stupidly thought, and even though I was constantly having to use a throat spray that day I somehow managed to struggle through the six songs that would make up our first demo. Unsurprisingly, the result was exactly what it was – someone trying to sing with their voice completely shot. At that time we didn't have a regular drummer so we hired a so-called session player for the paltry sum of £10. As the old saying goes, you only get what you pay for and that certainly came back to haunt us. He sounded more like a ten-bob drummer than a ten-pound drummer as his performance started badly and then got steadily worse. Even though there were obvious timing issues between him and the band, we had to go with what we had at the end of the day, as our budget wouldn't run to any more studio time.

More in hope than expectation, we sent the demo out to a few small labels. To say that I was gobsmacked when our lead guitarist Tim called me to say that two of the labels wanted us to come in so that they could hear some more of our stuff is putting it mildly. For God's sake, we hadn't even played a gig yet. Still, the excitement of somebody at a record company showing interest in your music is a feeling that's almost indescribable if you've never experienced it. Our first session was to be an acoustic one at a small label in that hotbed of music, Luton, so it was decided that Pete, our brand new drummer, would drive us to the studio in his van. However, Pete had failed to inform us that it had a leak in its exhaust pipe which meant that after a while, the exhaust fumes enveloped all of us inside the vehicle. Unfortunately I had drawn the short straw and had to sit in the back of the van with our gear while Pete and Tim sat up front, rather selfishly I thought, with both windows open and hankies tied around their mouths. The journey up the M1 seemed to go on forever, which resulted in the three of us suffering blinding headaches and waves of nausea – not exactly conducive our first attempt to break into the music business.

When we met the record company's A&R people, you could visibly see them wondering where the hell the reek of petrol was coming from. This embarrassment was taken to another level when Tim, who considered himself a bit of a George Peppard lookalike, a belief he constantly repeated to anyone he came into contact with, did something so shocking that it's a wonder they didn't throw us out of the studio on the spot. Suddenly Tim, in full view of our new prospective employers, struck a pose that Bruce Forsyth was known for on *The Generation Game*, namely bending over with a fist on his forehead, along with the bending of his left knee. He then proceeded to let one go. The noise was tremendous. There was a stunned silence after this vile explosion. This was only broken when Tim announced to everyone standing there, 'Hello. I'm Hunk Marvel, and this is my love call.' Not exactly a good start to our session and to this day, I have no idea why he did it. Thankfully, British reserve once again kicked in, and no further mention was made of his anal aberration that warm sunny evening in June 1980. Though our acoustic recording session went quite well, it came as no surprise that the label passed on us. A few weeks later we sadly found out that the other interested label had decided against signing a band who they said needed more development. I have to say they were spot on. The attention from those two labels came far too early.

In July 1980 we started gigging for the first time. I'd never played in front of a live audience before. It was a daunting prospect even though we had rent-a-crowd in attendance for most of the gigs. Though all of us felt the pressure before that first performance, as far as I was concerned, I was the one who was in the limelight. After all, they were my songs, and I was the lead vocalist and rhythm guitarist. If that wasn't bad enough, being a huge Elvis Costello fan, I had loved the way that he'd started his gig at the Hemel Pavilion back in 1978 when he came out on to the stage, on his own, to do a solo version of 'Chemistry Class'. How brilliant, I thought – just one man and his guitar. The impact of when the Attractions joined him on stage to tear into 'Mystery Dance' was stunning.

Now in rehearsals, we'd started our opening song with just me and my choppy, Costello-like rhythm guitar before the rest of the band came in. Unfortunately for me, the other group members thought this was a great idea and consequently I was faced with the prospect of standing there, horribly alone, with all eyes on me. The days leading up to that first gig were a nightmare. Stage fright plays horrible tricks on your imagination. What if I drop my plectrum? What if my mind goes blank? These scenarios were almost driving me mad with nerves. I can actually remember sitting on a park bench on the day of our first gig wondering how on earth I was going to get through that trial that night. The minutes seemed to drag before we were due to go on stage. But the strange thing with stage fright is that the thought of what you're going to do disappears as soon as you start playing. I managed to get through that first verse on my own with no mishaps. Having said that, I felt an overwhelming sense of relief when the rest of the band came in for the chorus. I've done hundreds of gigs now, played at the Dominion Theatre on Tottenham Court Road, Fairfield Hall in Croydon and the Marquee, just to name a few, and though the nerves never totally go away, after a time you just learn to control them.

Though the camaraderie when playing football with your mates is brilliant, it doesn't really compare with being in a band – not just the playing and recording side of it, but the social life is hard to beat, especially after a successful gig when the adrenaline mixed with alcohol can lead to a brilliant end to what had already been a memorable night. On one such occasion, after a gig in Watford, we all got stuck into the booze. Suddenly a plan was hatched to drive round to our ex-keyboard player's home, where we would throw stones at his bedroom window to get his attention and then moon en masse. Back in those days there was a peculiar craze for mooning which consisted of blokes sticking their bare arses out of car windows to shock innocent bystanders. After mooning at a line of people at a bus stop in Watford high street, we made our way down a country lane. I have to say that I hadn't previously participated in this practice; not even a considerable amount of alcohol could puncture my English reserve. Our drummer had also failed to take part. That said, he decided to give it a go when we were driving down that deserted country lane. Seeing that it was late at night, I've often wondered what his reasoning was but he was determined to join in the fun. He then wound down the rear window and proceeded to shove his bare backside into the cool evening air. Bad idea. After a few seconds, he let out a scream and sat back in his seat quickly, pulling his pants and trousers up. It seemed we'd been driving too close to some thorn bushes which had whipped him across his arse, a fact that he found completely unfunny but left the rest of us in near hysterics.

Finally, we arrived at Jon's home. As it was after midnight, the house was in darkness. It was the same Jon who had earlier left his band to join up with me. What made it hard for me personally was that we had started the band and I found it difficult that he had left to pursue a romance with a girl who bore an uncanny resemblance to a distressed ostrich. Still, as they say, beauty is in the eye of the beholder, though to be honest he was stretching the point a bit to say the least. Quietly, we stood beneath Jon's bedroom. A few small stones were then softly thrown against the window. Before I had a chance to decide whether I was going to join in this ridiculous act, the window was flung open whereupon an irate bloke shouted down to us, 'What the fuck are you playing at? Piss off!'

It was then that we realised that we'd got the wrong house. It was Jon's next-door neighbour. Quickly, we leapt back into the car and started to drive up the road. You'd have thought by now that we would have learned our lesson, but you'd be wrong. As we came to the T-junction, a car drove past us with a girl driving and her boyfriend in the passenger seat. They stopped a short distance behind us and we could see that as soon as they'd parked up, they were kissing passionately. Tim said, 'Quick, turn the car round.'

Ray, our manager, turned the engine off and rolled down the incline to arrive alongside them. I think we all had a pretty good idea of what Tim was up to. This was confirmed when Tim started undoing his trousers, lowering his pants, and then winding the window down. Silently, we rolled closer to the couple in the car until we were level with the driver's side window, which being in the heat of summer, was wide open. So engrossed were the couple in their throes of passion that they were completely unaware of our presence. That was until the girl looked over her shoulder only to discover Tim's horrible, hairy arse staring into her face. Instantly, she screamed, and her boyfriend shouted, 'What the fuck is going on?'

This was the second time we'd heard that phrase in a matter of minutes. Worryingly, this was starting to become a habit. Quickly, Ray started the engine and we sped off into the night. When Tim enquired, 'What did she look like?' we replied, 'Not bad, as far as we could make out.'

'How about the boyfriend?' Tim asked. 'What was he like?'

I remarked, 'Well, let's put it like this – she actually asked what your arse was doing next Saturday.'

The last memory I have of that night is being dropped off at my home. I turned round to wave goodnight to the lads only to see Ray's car hurtling down the road in reverse. The night air was pierced by their lunatic, banzai screaming. Such antics would now be frowned upon with accusations of indecent exposure but back in those days you could get away with such behaviour. Within groups of young males, that was the norm rather than the exception.

To counter-balance any criticism I might receive for recounting this episode, which to the woke brigade must be truly shocking, I would add that unlike today, especially in big cities where knife crime is endemic among young men, I know which era I would have preferred to grow up in. To be that age now, in my view, would be horrific, where people communicate remotely instead of the face-to-face bonding that we enjoyed back in those days.

* * *

By the end of that year and at the beginning of 1981, the band had run its course. It's hard to keep a band together who are doing their own material especially since we'd had no further interest following our audition with the indie label back in the summer. In the end it was just me and our new keyboard player left. It was sad to lose everyone but thankfully, a year later, we reunited as mates rather than band members, and have retained our friendship ever since. I said to Tim a few years later that nothing ever came from being in that band, and he replied, 'Well, you're right. It was a shame but what a summer we had. One of the happiest of my life.'

And on reflection, I have to agree. They truly were halcyon days.

In June 1981 I'd signed my first music publishing deal at a small publishing company in London who paid me £300 as an advance. In 1981, that was a fair amount of money. Importantly, it was the first time that I'd been paid for making music. To say that I was ecstatic is an understatement, especially as that windfall I received meant that I could live like a king on our lads' holiday in Majorca a few weeks later. I wonder what that £300 would be worth in today's money? Listen, if you can get anyone in that cut-throat industry to financially back you, then that's some achievement. I heard once that the multitude of bands and songwriters who are actually signed to a label is a tiny six per cent, so I consider myself fortunate that I've had various recording and publishing deals right up to the present day. One last word on the music business – during that time, it must have been a year later, another production company offered me £250 to buy one of my songs. Brilliant, I thought. More money. Thankfully, even though I was naive in business matters, I did have the presence of mind to ask what 'buy' actually meant. The A&R bloke on the other end of the phone suddenly became defensive. Eventually I forced him to come clean and learned that by selling that song for £250, I would waive any monies earned on it, forever. You won't be surprised to learn that I declined their offer and said thanks, but no thanks. It was a salutary lesson of how record labels and the like will prey on those new to the business.

* * *

It's easy to look back now, as they say, in hindsight with 20/20 vision, but I had an uneasy feeling that the 1980/81 season would be a long, hard one for the Blues. To have missed out on promotion that previous season by the narrowest of margins right at the death meant it would be a difficult task for manager Geoff Hurst when it came to galvanising the players and the fans for another promotion push. To my surprise we sold striker Tommy Langley to QPR for £400,000 in early August, a decision I found to be baffling all round. For though Langley was not the most skilful centre-forward seen at the Bridge, he was a regular goalscorer and his work rate and tireless running had earned him the nickname of 'Lungs' among his team mates. And what on earth were we doing selling him to one of our rivals for promotion? It didn't make sense but obviously Hurst had other ideas and was pinning all of his hopes on Colin Lee, who had frequently been out injured and had managed only one league goal since his arrival from Spurs, all of which made the decision to part with Langley even more perplexing. It was almost written in the stars that when QPR visited the Bridge a couple of weeks later in the league, Langley would score their goal in the 1-1 draw. If that wasn't bad enough, when Chelsea played the return fixture at Loftus Road later in the season, guess who scored the goal in their 1-0 victory? Langley had pointedly stuck two fingers up to his ex-boss who saw him, as they say, as surplus to requirements.

The purpose of this book is to recount the two pivotal campaigns of 1982/83 and 1983/84, and though I have gone into some detail of the season that never was, 1979/80, to analyse what happened over the next couple of years would be as depressing to read as having to sit down and plough through the complete works of Dostoevsky, or being forced to watch every film that Ingmar Bergman ever made. Not to put too fine a point on it, the next two years were truly abysmal. Of course there were a few bright spots, like the unlikely win over Liverpool at the Bridge in the fifth round of the FA Cup in February 1982, which at the time was a massive shock as Liverpool were still dominating football both here and in Europe. Any joy that this result brought to the Blues faithful was extinguished when we lost to Spurs in the quarter-finals, our first appearance in that stage of the competition for 12 years. Although Mike Fillery had blasted an unstoppable free kick past Ray Clemence to give the Blues a half-time lead, after the break Spurs fought back with three quickfire goals to take control. And even though Alan Mayes halved the deficit, there was sadly no doubt about the difference in class between the two sides. And I don't have to tell any Chelsea fan how hard that is for me to admit.

We also pulled off another giant-killing act in October 1981 when we knocked out Southampton, Kevin Keegan and all, 2-1 after extra time at the Bridge, following a 1-1 draw at The Dell. Even this joy was short-lived because in the next round we surrendered meekly to lowly Wigan, 4-2.

Chapter 9

By the autumn of 1980, Chelsea looked set once again for a promotion challenge after fine performances against Watford at Vicarage Road where the Blues came away as 3-2 winners, followed by the thrashing of Newcastle at the Bridge where the Geordies were buried beneath an avalanche of goals as the Blues hit six without reply. In fact the brilliant team goal scored by Gary Chivers is often cited as being one of the most memorable goals of that particular campaign.

By early November the Blues found themselves second in the league. All looked promising but how quickly things can turn. Chelsea's goal at Notts County, which earned a well-deserved draw, was unbelievably the last goal that they would score on the road for the rest of the season. Little did we know that John Bumstead's 84th-minute equaliser at Meadow Lane would be as good as it got for the massive Chelsea away support that season. One new signing who hit the ground running was Phil Driver, who had come from Wimbledon. He looked to be an exciting prospect; a fast, tricky winger. But yet again that promise never quite materialised, and Driver soon disappeared from prominence.

A few years later, Driver turned up at a training session for one of the teams I played for. Unfortunately I wasn't there that night but according to those who were present, nobody could get near him which just shows you the gulf that exists between the amateurs and the pros. Even those players who you don't rate are, in truth, on another level to anything you might face on a Sunday morning. Just remember, they have gone through a system where only one per cent of boys are lucky enough to ever have a career as a professional footballer, which is a frightening and sobering statistic when you think about it. As the old saying goes, many are called but few are chosen.

10

THE CURTAIN came down on 1980/81 when Notts County put the final nail into the coffin of what had been a dismal season. The visitors' 2-0 win confirmed their promotion to the top flight while Chelsea had finished in a miserable 12th place. Manager Geoff Hurst had already been sacked just before that final home game, leaving his assistant Bobby Gould in charge for his one and only match as the Chelsea boss. Talk about the lunatics taking over the asylum. Gould's shortcomings as a player were still starkly evident when he went into management; a mixture of hard endeavour coupled with bluster and bullshit. I wasn't exactly heartbroken to see the back of Geoff Hurst either. In my eyes, he never got the club. Well, why should he? He spent the majority of his career at London rivals West Ham and I should imagine that Chelsea held no special place in his heart. In retrospect, I think it was a big mistake retaining his services after narrowly missing out on promotion in 1979/80. By the start of the following campaign it soon became evident that the Hurst/Gould management team was indeed a busted flush.

To add insult to injury, Neil Warnock, the Notts County boss, actually turned down the Chelsea job that summer, and who could have blamed him? His County side were heading for the First Division while the Blues were nothing more than a mid-table Second Division team. The anger at the board of directors' incompetence was evident that day at the Bridge with a pitch invasion which had the home fans calling for the Mears family, who had run the club since its birth, to do the honourable thing and exit stage left sooner rather than later. Little did we know that bleak afternoon that it wouldn't be until the spring of 1982 that our saviour, businessman Ken Bates, would enter the picture. Bates, who despite being a figure who courted controversy on a weekly basis, is the main reason why Chelsea Football Club still exists to this day as one of the most successful sides in Europe.

Shortly after that protest, Chelsea fans got their wish when chairman Brian Mears stepped down from his position in a move that ended the Mears dynasty, which was by now well past its sell-by date. It was evident that the club needed a shake-up and Bates, who'd parted with £1 for the right to take over, would have been under no illusions about the momentous task he faced. There was a joke going around the club at that time that when Bates had handed the pound note over, he asked for change – a comment that was devoured by supporters of rival clubs.

The club's first task after the sacking of Geoff Hurst would be to appoint a new manager. Many names were mentioned. Would we go for a big name again? Well, no, not really. The appointment of John Neal hardly raised pulses around Stamford Bridge. True, when he'd been at Wrexham and Middlesbrough, he'd built good, solid sides. Like many Blues fans I was somewhat underwhelmed by Neal's appointment, but what a masterstroke it was in retrospect.

Progress on the field, however, was slow. The 1981/82 season was, in all honesty, forgettable; apart from the victory over Southampton in the League Cup and the run to the

FA Cup quarter-finals, there was very little to cheer about. The nadir of these times was without question the two games against those giants of football, Rotherham United. I was in a recording studio when the Blues travelled to Millmoor on the last day of October 1981. Privately, I was quietly confident that we'd get something out of this game, a belief engendered by our giant-killing of Southampton the previous Wednesday. I can clearly recall going into the restroom in the studio to see how we had fared that fateful day. Nothing, however, prepared me for the video printer display that showed the scoreline of Rotherham 6 Chelsea 0. I could feel my face flushing hot much to the amusement of the other people in the lounge. Yet again I had that sinking feeling in the pit of my stomach, which still exists today whenever the Blues lose a game. But this day was the lowest of the low. I even felt my eyes brimming with tears. Unable to control my emotions, I beat a hasty retreat from the lounge to the relative safety of the car park where I could wallow in my own misery at leisure.

What had happened to the club that I'd started supporting in 1967? Those days of cup finals and European nights now seemed to be a lifetime away. But, despite all of this, those of us who endured those times were even more fervent in our support. Who cared that we were a sleeping giant, as the media were only too happy to point out? Let's be honest, a sleeping giant was a gross understatement – more like a giant in a coma, in the IC unit.

* * *

One game that always remains a cherished memory is the Boxing Day 1981 fixture against QPR at Loftus Road. Though Rangers reached the FA Cup Final that season, Chelsea were the living embodiment of Scrooge that day as we showed no Christmas spirit to our local neighbours, coming away with a brilliant – if unexpected – 2-0 win. There were just 12 minutes left when Clive Walker broke the deadlock with a low drive past Rangers keeper John Burridge, to give the Blues the lead, who that day were playing in a fantastic all-yellow strip. The win was completed when in the 88th minute, Alan Mayes's volley secured the points.

If anyone ever tells you that Chelsea had no support back in those days, I would advise you to check out the YouTube video of that game. The end where Chelsea scored their two goals is packed to the rafters with a huge visiting following, wildly celebrating our victory over our more sedate, passive near neighbours. I was there and I find it hard to believe that you could ever find a more passionate crowd than the Chelsea away following in those days. It seemed that the club's adversity bred an almost biblical fervour among its followers.

You would have imagined that after such a brilliant result, when Rotherham visited the Bridge a few weeks later, the Blues would have exacted revenge on the Yorkshire club for what had almost certainly been one of the lowest moments in their history. On the Wednesday before Rotherham's visit we'd lost at home, yet again, to Crystal Palace after falling behind to two early goals, the second of which was scored by Jerry Murphy, who would a few years later sign for the Blues. Actually, I can't remember when we signed him, or when he left. It seemed to me that one day he was there and the next day he was gone. However, I did have the pleasure of sitting on a seat opposite him on the tube to Fulham Broadway on the day of the match, which he duly played in.

It's hard to imagine any of today's cosseted players travelling to the game on public transport, but these were different times. I recognised Jerry at once but let me tell you that there were other Chelsea supporters in that carriage who I'm convinced didn't have a clue. That period of the early 1980s was strange days indeed. Some of the players who turned out for the club have been all but forgotten. Who remembers Spurs flop Mark Falco's three games for us in 1982/83? Not many, I suspect. The very same Mark Falco who had been preferred over a young Kerry Dixon at Spurs when Falco was offered a pro contract and Kerry was mercilessly shown the door to ply his trade in the lower divisions with the likes of Reading. Still, as it turned out, Spurs' loss was definitely Chelsea's gain when just a few years later, Dixon's arrival would herald a massive upturn in the Blues' fortunes.

* * *

As for the music, by Christmas 1982 we had two female singers in the band, one of whom I would start to go out with the following spring. But more of that later. Lynn, the younger of the pair, invited us to a private party at a pub in Dunstable during the festive holidays. While I was dancing with her, she said to me, 'You like football, don't you?'

'Slightly,' was my somewhat glib reply.

'Well, you see that blond-haired bloke at the bar – that's Kerry Dixon.'

'Oh,' I remarked, thinking to myself, 'Who the fuck is Kerry Dixon?'

'He plays for Reading,' Lynn went on to say.

So bloody what, I thought. Little did I know how much of an impact he was going to play in my life over the next few years.

Just 12 months later, Dixon was firmly established as one of the best strikers in the country, forming a deadly partnership with David Speedie, one of the greatest forward pairings in the Blues' history. I don't know if my mind is playing tricks with me but I seem to recall buying a newspaper in WH Smith in Watford, in what must have been late 1982 or early 1983, and reading an article that reported that a certain Charlie George was training with the Blues. Surely not, I thought, yet I have to admit that I was thrilled at the prospect, even though by this time George would have been in his early 30s, which was considered ancient in footballing terms in those days. The prospect of having the bloke who scored that iconic goal in the 1971 FA Cup Final against Liverpool was something that fired my imagination. George's career never reached the heights that we'd expected after he secured the Double for Arsenal, but his celebration of laying down on his back after his 20-yard screamer had flown past Ray Clemence was copied on local football pitches the length and breadth of the country by kids, who for one brief moment, could somehow dream of scoring the winning goal in the FA Cup Final. Yet again, nothing came of this rumour, and George carried on in his nomadic career until the end of his playing days.

* * *

On Saturday, 20 March 1982, I took up my usual place in front of the tea bar at the Bridge. It was no longer packed to capacity like it used to be when I first went back in the 1968/69 season. Now, depressingly, there was plenty of room. That old joke comes to mind of, 'Where did you stand?' 'Next to the other bloke.' Another favourite jibe aimed towards me was that Chelsea didn't have a Spot the Ball competition – they had Spot the Crowd. These were similar barbs that I had inflicted on my mates who supported my local team, Watford, in the Blues' glory days of the early 1970s. Now these insults were thrown back in my face. Still, if you dish it out, I suppose you have to take it back, though it was undoubtedly a bitter pill to swallow.

Yet that day against Rotherham would be our chance to put them in their place. The memory of that 6-0 hammering was still fresh in the minds of everyone connected with Chelsea. All of us on the terraces that day were praying that our desire for revenge would be matched on the pitch by the 11 men who wore blue, the 11 men who carried our hopes that afternoon. After 23 minutes we'd taken our first step in retribution when spindly legged winger Peter Rhoades-Brown put us 1-0 ahead. Looking back, what an unlikely surname that was for a footballer – Rhoades-Brown. I couldn't get it out of my head that he came from an upper-class background, spending his time attending debs coming-out parties, punting on the rivers that flowed through the dreaming spires of Oxford, and having a man servant who went by the name of Jeeves.

Our joy at the Blues taking the lead was quickly extinguished when Rotherham levelled just five minutes later, through Billy McEwan, and by half-time the visitors led 3-1. At the interval the stark reality hit every Blues fan in attendance that their club was being humbled by a team that had spent their entire history within the lower ranks of football in this country. Though Chelsea made attempts to reduce the deficit, nothing came of them, and to add insult to injury Rotherham plunged the knife even deeper when they scored a fourth goal in the last minute. When the final whistle blew, it was a welcome relief that we didn't have to endure the agony of that desperate affair for one second longer. There it was: Chelsea 1, Rotherham United 4. The stark reality was that over those two games that season, the aggregate scoreline was 10-1 in favour of our less than glorious rivals. But the final nail in the coffin was the fact that Rotherham were managed for those two games by none other than my old friend Emlyn Hughes.

What a walk back to Victoria station I endured that evening. I stopped off for a drink at the King's Head and Eight Bells, but even that tasted bitter. Chelsea played out the rest of the season with mixed results; a couple of back-to-back derby wins against Crystal Palace and QPR brought some light into the darkness but I'm sure, like everyone else connected with the club, we were all eager to get this bloody, interminable season over with. When the curtain came down on Saturday, 15 May following a 1-1 draw against Blackburn at Ewood Park, the fact was that for the second season running, we'd finished nowhere, stuck in mid-table in 12th place. Still, like every supporter, a new campaign brings new hope. Surely next season would have to be better. Surely? Little did we know that 1982/83 would see Chelsea, who had been teetering on the brink for the last couple of years, almost fall into the dark pit of an abyss that would be almost impossible to return from.

11

ME AND my mates used to play five-a-side on a Sunday night at the local leisure centre, a ritual that had been taking place for almost a decade. These games were always fiercely competitive. From my personal point of view, my credo was that though they might be my mates, that was in no way going to stop me kicking them into the middle of next week. When I was a kid my uncle Joey, who was a really decent player and a Chelsea fan to boot, said to me, 'Never change your game whether it's a kickaround or a proper game. Set your standard, and never let your performance slip no matter how innocuous the game is.'

Most weeks, the matches were hard but fair but in the August of 1980, one particular Sunday evening, for some unknown reason that night turned into nothing short of all-out war. My bandmates were playing that night and I was to be on the opposite side against my own musical colleagues. The majority of our side was made up from our old street team, Avenue, who we'd all played for in the early 1970s. Where the trouble started, I have no idea. Perhaps a mistimed tackle might have been the flashpoint but before very long the mood was turning decidedly ugly.

My first involvement in the proceedings was to trip my best mate, Mick, as he went clean through and was bearing down on goal. I purposely clipped the back of his heel which sent him tumbling forwards, such was the speed that he was running at. This led to Mick having to do a head-over-heels on the hard, unforgiving gymnasium floor. Mick was a mild-mannered bloke and indeed, as I have said, one of the best friends I've ever had. To my shame, my dastardly actions provoked Mick into squaring up to me with both of his fists clenched. I knew that I'd done wrong but was I going to let him know that? No. I just shoved him away and gave him an icy stare. This litany of kicking and fouling carried on. I was tackled so hard that night by my mate Bob that he split my training shoe away from its sole. Then there was another occasion when I was about to hit a bouncing ball towards goal when Bob unbelievably headed the ball off my foot. A split-second later and it would have been debatable as to whether Bob's head, or the ball, ended up in the back of the net.

Next on my hit list was Pete, our drummer, a friend I still have to this day. But that didn't stop me from hacking him to the ground with a vicious tackle from behind. Yet again, I found myself being squared up to by one of my best mates. Once again, I was questioned with, 'What the fuck are you playing at?' My attitude towards him was one of total disinterest and I met his entreaties to calm down with a dead-eyed stare. I would like to point out that I wasn't the only one trying to recreate that infamous 1970 FA Cup Final replay at Old Trafford between Chelsea and Leeds, which is considered to be one of the most brutal games ever seen in this country. Just like that night, everyone present on that Sunday evening seemed to be intent on getting stuck in.

My next flare-up came when I was shielding the ball against the wall of the five-a-side pitch. Andy, one of the opposition players who I never got on with over the years, suddenly realised that here was his chance for revenge for all the shit I'd dished out to him over those years by kicking me in the back of my legs with a pitiless fury. I instantly picked the ball up and asked him yet again, the same old question of what the fuck he was playing at! His response was to sneer at me and turn his back. Big mistake. I then hurled the ball at the back of his head. The inevitable outcome of this act was that we had to be pulled apart by both teams. It is no wonder that among my mates, that game back in August 1980 was forever known as Bloody Sunday.

Then came the two incidents that were to have long-term repercussions on me personally. Ray, who was the band's unofficial manager – he booked some gigs for us and also ferried us around – was in fairness a pretty stylish player. On that night we were on opposing sides. As was normal, everyone had to take a turn in goal under the rule of 'one goal and in', and now it was my turn between the sticks. I'd always done well in goal and was determined not to let a soft one in, as some people obviously did so that they could get back out on the pitch. I'd made a couple of decent saves and all seemed to be going pretty well. That was until Ray sent a screaming shot past me that hit the back of the net like a bullet. I hadn't even moved, such was the power of Ray's effort. Fair enough, it was a great goal, but it caused the red mist to descend in front of my eyes. I clearly heard Ray mumble, 'Pick that one out, you fucker.' Suddenly I had that feeling you get when you drive over a humpback bridge, like your stomach has fallen alarmingly to the soles of your feet. To put it mildly, I was seething and hell-bent on revenge. The chance of retribution was not long in coming as Ray was now taking his turn in goal for our opponents. Suddenly, the ball was squared back to me, and from a few yards out I could hardly miss. Ray was out of position on the other side of the goal. All I had to do was just roll the ball into an empty net. But not me – oh, not me. Instead, I trapped the ball in the hope that Ray would make a last-ditch, valiant effort to block my shot, which is exactly what happened as he dived to save what looked like a certain goal. Instead of just side-footing the ball past him I blasted it straight at him, the result being that it hit him on the side of his head before ricocheting into the back of the net. Revenge, as they say, is a dish best served cold. The side of Ray's face now had a bloody big red mark where the ball had smashed into his skull. To say that he was not best pleased would be a gross understatement.

You'd think that the honours were even, that I'd just leave it there, which would have been the sensible thing to do. But that night, common sense was the one thing that was thrown out of the window. The incident that put a stop on my playing football, or any other sport for six long months, happened in the last few minutes of the game, and again it was a clash with Ray. As I previously mentioned, Ray was a really decent player and fancied himself a bit. When the ball was thrown out to him by their keeper, Ray did his best impression of Franz Beckenbauer, the imperious German World Cup-winning captain. He put his foot on the ball while he casually considered his options of who to pass to. Again, the red mist descended. Who the fuck did he think he was? And consequently, I decided in an instant that I was going to clean him out.

Like a lunatic, I threw myself into a sliding tackle which, let me tell you, is not the done thing in five-a-side football. My outstretched left leg connected with the ball in the very instant that Ray, who by this time was already sick to death of my antics, decided to kick it away with as much venom as he was physically capable of. The result was that my left foot, which was fully extended, took the full force of Ray's clearance. The pain was like a red-hot poker as my left knee seemed to be in a very strange position. But, this being back in the day when tackling like this was nothing out of the ordinary, we both just got on with the game, even though I was reduced to hobbling around on one leg for the few remaining minutes. Strangely, the pain subsided and I thought, wrongly, that I'd got away with trying to cripple myself. The mood in the bar was muted, especially towards yours truly. Some of my victims could hardly bear to look at me, let alone talk to me.

To make things even more awkward, Ray and Tim were due to give me a lift home. I had expected them to tell me to get lost. The silence in the car was deafening. When we arrived at my home, Tim, who was sitting up front with Ray, got out and pushed up the passenger seat to let me out of the car. As I turned around to say thanks for the lift, I heard Ray mutter under his breath, 'Just fuck off,' and to be honest, who could blame him.

The first sign that I'd done myself some serious damage became apparent when I woke up with a searing hot pain in the side of my left knee. I went down the stairs to put on an ice pack and there, upon inspection, I saw that the said knee was inflamed and swollen. It didn't look good, and for the next few days I was hobbling around with no sign of improvement.

Finally I gave in and went to see my GP who unbelievably thought that the best solution was to strap up my knee to the point where I couldn't even bend it. During the next month, I had a few attempts at returning to the Sunday team I was playing for at the time, Orion, but there was nothing stellar about this lot. On both occasions I lasted until I had the first touch of the ball whereupon my left knee would give way, leaving me in a heap on the ground. After the second attempt at a comeback, our winger said to me, 'Have you tried the remedial physiotherapy team?' This was run out of our local sports centre. Apparently, he knew someone who'd had a similar injury and the physios had managed to get him playing again.

Consequently, I booked an appointment with the head physio, a fearsome woman who looked and acted like a sergeant major. Straightaway, she said to me, 'Who the hell strapped your leg up?'

Meekly, I replied, 'It was my GP.'

'Well, he's a bloody idiot. This will only cause muscle wastage,' she said, and removed the strapping to examine my knee, which by now looked very sorry for itself. She then announced, 'I'm going to run an ultrasound over your knee to see if there are any tears. Believe me, you're going to feel it.'

Worryingly, she said all of this with an unhealthy amount of glee. Sure enough, after a little bit of probing, she found the problem. A sharp pain shot through my knee.

'It's a small tear in the lateral ligament,' she announced.

What the bloody hell was a lateral ligament, I thought. Sadly, over the next six months, I would become extremely well-versed in that subject.

'When can I play again?' was my instant question. Her reply to a 24-year-old who lived for playing football was quite chilling.

'That's if you play again,' she coldly said.

Jesus, I thought. A life without football. Though I loved following Chelsea, nothing can replicate the thrill of actually playing the game yourself, no matter what standard you play at.

'However,' she went on, 'if you work hard, and come to our sessions in the gym at the Watford hospital once a week, you could be playing again in six months.'

Six months? Six months – I could hardly believe it! I could hardly take in what she was talking about. Building up the muscle in the knee, she informed me, would help the small tear to heal.

Relieved, I said, 'Yes, I'm up for that.'

And so for the next six long months I went to the remedial classes and carried out my exercises religiously. For somebody who had played a lot of sport, including badminton and swimming, as well as football, it was a deeply bleak six months. It still amazes me to this day that those remedial classes were full of young blokes like myself, trying to get fit to play the game they loved, not for any financial reward, just with a passion to get out there, back on the pitch every Saturday or Sunday.

I sometimes wonder if that desire is still evident in blokes of the same age in present times. There are more distractions, and football, to this generation in my opinion, is not held with as much fervour as we displayed back in the day. I would hate to be in my mid-20s at the time of writing in 2023. It seems that the birth of the internet has led to a lot of young people leading solitary lives where their circle of friends can be mainly found online. I recently drove past a football pitch in St Helens on the Isle of Wight where I now live. It was a beautiful sunny day, slap, bang in the middle of the school holidays. There it was, the grass that looked so inviting, standing empty, completely empty, not a soul in sight. How different that would have been back in my era, when I'm almost certain that a game would have been going on between local kids, and a few from further afield who had just asked if they could join in. Sadly, it seems as though those days are a thing of the past, and the lure of the gaming console, the internet and incredibly, their phones, seems to be the preoccupation of teenagers right now. You could say that it's a generational thing, but I really pity the kids of today who will never have the sense of freedom that kids growing up in the 1960s and '70s enjoyed, where it was down to yourselves to provide your own entertainment, an ethos that encouraged creativity and imagination.

In March 1981 I was finally fit enough to make my first appearance after six tedious months. Though the remedial gym had been tough, it seemed that all of that hard work had paid off. I even managed to score eight goals in the remaining games of that season. After that injury, I never played another match without a knee support. I didn't really need it but to me, it was some type of physical and mental crutch, and made me feel safe. One memory I have of those days is the phone calls I used to make from my office on a Monday morning, when I wanted to find out which of my friends was still talking to me. Not that I was the only one who practised some of the game's dark arts, but to my credit, in my mind at least, I had a conscience.

12

IAN HUTCHINSON is my favourite ever Chelsea player. Hutch started out as a defender before Dave Sexton saw his potential as a striker, a move of incredible insight, as he went on to become the idol of thousands of Blues fans with his all-out, bustling style of play. Hutch had the heart of a lion and would put himself through hell and high water for the cause. So I decided, although I could never match Hutch's ability, that in my own modest way I would try to match the passion and endeavour that he displayed every time he pulled on the royal blue shirt. You have to remember that the game I described over the last few pages was seen as perfectly acceptable back in those days. I've no doubt that myself and my mates would be given our marching orders many times over today where, in my eyes, it seems that if you look at somebody the wrong way, it can easily result in a booking or a dismissal.

In my opinion, the incident that cost us the 2020 FA Cup Final against Arsenal was the sending-off of Mateo Kovačić. It was a ludicrous decision to give Kovačić a second yellow card when, as it turned out, the slow-motion replay showed that he had actually been the player who was fouled, and not his Arsenal opponent. We also have VAR to contend with, a new technology that has sucked all the joy out of the game. When the Blues score now,

I always wait before I celebrate the goal in case one of the players' toenails was slightly offside. Football is a game played by human beings, refereed by human beings (though sometimes I have my doubts), so it follows that there is a chance of human error and I preferred it that way. Sometimes the decisions went for your team and sometimes they didn't. It was all part of the game. Now there is that agonising wait for the VAR check before you can be sure that your team has actually scored. It's my belief that the magical quality has been lost from our national game, a magic that will be lost forever unless the football authorities decide to give up on VAR as a bad job, which in my view, it most definitely is.

* * *

The summer of 1982 would have faded away in most people's memories if not for one seismic event. For the first time in my life, Britain was at war. Yes, I know it was officially known as the Falklands Conflict, and for some strange reason we were not allowed to call it a war, as 'conflict' I suppose was more politically correct. But if you have two countries' armies trying to kill each other, then in my book that's war. The Falklands had been a sore point for Argentina, who claimed that the islands – or the Malvinas, as they called them – belonged to them.

I can remember sitting in a pub one night when Steve, who was in the Navy Reserve, told us chillingly that the government were drawing up lists of who would be drafted if the conflict spread to the Argentine mainland. As all of us were in our mid-20s this was a terrifying prospect. Yet, once again, the gallows humour that makes up the British psyche was lying in wait when I said to Steve, 'So, you're in the Navy Reserve then?'

'That's right,' he replied with a sense of pride.

'But you can't fucking swim,' I snapped back much to the amusement of my mates. Steve looked crestfallen. Before he could offer a protest, I hit him with a second shot, 'I suppose you could always ask for a rubber ring if the worst came to the worst.' Poor old Steve was speechless. One of the loudest laughs at this joke was coming from our drummer, Pete.

'What are you laughing at?' I enquired.

'What do you mean?' Pete asked.

'Well, you're three years younger than the rest of us. You'll be in an earlier draft than us.'

The colour drained from his face.

'But I can't go. I've got work,' he pleaded.

'Sorry, Pete,' my mate Tim said. 'If you've got to go – you've got to go.'

'But what could I do? I'm just a drummer,' said Pete in a panicked voice.

'Well,' Tim said, 'seeing that you're a drummer, you could be in charge of the big bass drum and lead the charge up the beach when we invade. How would you feel about that?'

'That's not funny,' Pete snapped back among the hysterical laughter from the rest of us.

* * *

During one of our visits to Dave's bungalow in Brixham in the early summer of 1982, five of us went out for an evening of high excitement and drinking in the rather staid, classically English seaside resort of Torquay, which the British Tourist Board would have you believe was part of the English Riviera. After our pub crawl, which in truth was pretty tame, we decided to end the evening by taking part in that great British tradition of all groups of English lads together on the beer – to round off the night with a curry. By this time, we were all ravenously hungry, discovering yet again that there's nothing like a night of drinking to increase your appetite for what has now become one of the UK's traditional meals. As you can imagine, finding a curry house in genteel Torquay was no easy task, but eventually we discovered one quite close to the pier, if my memory serves me correctly. We'd hardly gone through the door when the manager of the establishment told us, 'Sorry, boys. We're full up.' And he was right. The place was packed with people who'd had the same idea as us. Deflated, we congregated outside to discuss what our next move should be in our quest for late-night food, when, much to our surprise, Chas and Dave and their drummer, Micky, walked round the corner. This was during their heyday and they'd just had a big hit with 'Ain't No Pleasing You', so I suppose the reason for them being in Torquay was either a one-off gig, or a summer season.

'Evening, lads,' they said as they made their way into the restaurant.

'It's full,' we said.

'Oh, really?' said Chas. 'We'll see about that.'

And with that, they entered while we were still wondering how the hell we were going to find some food that night.

Then we heard muffled shouting coming from inside the restaurant. All of a sudden, the door was flung open and out came the trio. They all looked apoplectic with rage. I can't remember if it was Chas or Dave, or even Micky, but one of them shouted back into the packed restaurant, 'You can stick your curry up your fucking arse!'

This made it quite obvious that their plea of 'do you know who we are?' had fallen on deaf ears.

As surreal moments go, it's certainly right up there. I can still picture the three of them storming off into the night, muttering obscenities. I've often wondered if they ever found somewhere to eat that night. I know we didn't and instead made our way back to Dave's bungalow in Brixham where we decided to fall back on that old classic, fried egg sandwiches, which was the go-to late-night snack for countless numbers of young blokes back in those days.

* * *

Later on in that summer of 1982, Chelsea signed the 36-year-old Brian 'Pop' Robson. We'd also made a bid for Joey Jones of Wrexham but our offer was turned down, only for the Blues to go back a short while later and finally get their man. Another inspired signing was Darlington's David Speedie, a firebrand little forward who, despite his lack of inches, was brilliant in the air. Pop Robson was very much in the senior-pro category. But to tell you the truth, Pop looked more like a man of 56 rather than someone 20 years younger, largely due to the fact that he started losing his hair in his early 20s. Despite his follicular problems, I'd always thought that he was a fantastic goalscorer. He'd been part of the Newcastle side that won the Inter-Cities Fairs Cup in 1969 and had later played for West Ham. I'd seen him play quite a few times as some of my mates supported the Hammers. Back in those days, if there was nothing to do on a Saturday afternoon with the Blues playing away, I'd tag along to Upton Park. Don't get me wrong, I have no affiliation with West Ham, but it was better than staying at home kicking your heels, waiting for Chelsea's result to come in on BBC's *Grandstand* or ITV's *World of Sport*. Believe me, if my mates had been Spurs supporters, there is no way that I would have joined them. There was no way I was giving that lot my money. Attending a basket-weaving convention, to me, would have been a preferable option. So, all in all, I was chuffed that we'd managed to sign Pop in the twilight of his career, because the proof was plain to see. He definitely knew where the back of the net was.

When Chelsea visited Cambridge United for the opening fixture of the 1982/83 season, I was camping with my mates down in Hayle, Cornwall, and my God, what a weird place that was. When we arrived in the tiny village, we called into the local convenience store to stock up on supplies before heading to the campsite. The convenience store resembled an old barn. As we were purchasing our stuff, I suddenly noticed World War Two Nazi uniforms up on the wall above the shelves of produce, and, incredibly they were, in some form of twisted reality, for sale.

Like a lot of blokes of my generation, I was fascinated by the Germans in World War Two. In fact, when we played at being soldiers back in the 1960s, no one wanted to be British. All of us wanted to be the Germans. I suppose it was something to do with their uniforms which were very stylish, while our poor Tommies wore outfits that looked like they'd been plundered from a jumble sale. Mind you, you had to be careful about showing too much interest in the Nazis, as back in the 1960s it was barely 20 years since the war had ended, tensions were still running high, and the memories of that conflict were still red raw. To be called a German-lover by your mates was still one of the biggest insults that could be aimed at you. I definitely had to curb my fascination with everything to do with the Nazis seeing that most of my family had lived through the Blitz, and also I had a couple of uncles who'd been in the Eighth Army during the North African campaign in the Western Desert. Of course, we were just kids and knew nothing about the atrocities perpetrated by the most evil death cult in world history.

My best bet is that these uniforms in the convenience store must have been left behind by some film company as, at a push, the nearby beaches could be taken for being the Normandy beaches on D-Day. Though I was tempted, at the age of 26 there was no way that I was going to buy any Nazi regalia. As well as the uniforms, the walls above the shelves were also adorned with Nazi flags, also for sale. I half expected there to be a special two for one offer on Iron Crosses when we reached the checkout. I thought about asking the cashier what was going on, but he looked like something out of the film *Deliverance* and had an expression on his face that seemed to say, 'I only have two brain cells, and one of them is on the blink.'

* * *

That afternoon we crowded into Les's car to keep up with the football scores on his car radio. At half-time Chelsea were drawing 0-0 with Cambridge. Oh, well, I thought. I'll take a point on the opening day. I can't remember what the live commentary was, but no updates about the Blues were given during the second half, which is hardly surprising, I suppose, as Cambridge United versus Chelsea in the Second Division was not exactly a fixture that fired your imagination, which highlighted just how far we had fallen in the eyes of the footballing family.

Then came the dreaded wait for the classified results at five o'clock. In a sonorous voice, the BBC announcer reported that Chelsea had won 1-0 thanks to a goal by debutant Pop Robson three minutes from time. I was ecstatic. Perhaps this would be our season. Visions of glory danced before my eyes. Could there be a promotion push led by our veteran striker? Such are the hopes of every football supporter at the dawn of a new season where whatever happened in the previous campaign was now a thing of the past. If I'd only known what 1982/83 would bring, I would have celebrated that opening-day fixture even more fervently as there was very little to get excited about over the coming months. Slowly but surely, the season descended into what was nothing short of a disaster.

That night we went to the local pub where we were blithely ignored by the regulars, as were all of the other holidaymakers in the bar. In fact the only eye contact made was when one of the locals would give you a murderous look that seemed to say, 'We don't take kindly to strangers around these parts.' Still, who cared? I was in a good mood. Chelsea had won and it had been a brilliantly sunny day. There's nothing like an away win on the opening weekend to raise the spirits. Not even the prospect of sharing a two-man tent with Mick could dampen my feeling of bonhomie.

To say that the campsite was basic is putting it mildly. The plot where we'd pitched our tent was quite a distance away from the camp toilets. These toilets were in a rundown edifice with a freezing, cold-stone floor. The aroma of the blocks of disinfectant in the urinals, coupled with the bitter stench of stale piss, made the thought of a visit to these facilities, apart from in an extreme emergency, unthinkable. This resulted in the hedge behind our tents receiving a regular watering.

After saying goodnight to the other lads, Mick and I returned to our tent. Both of us were readers so we set up a small light between our sleeping bags so that we could at least get stuck into our books. A short while later, we heard movement from the other tent that our mates were sleeping in.

'What's that?' Mick said.

'It's just one of the boys taking a piss,' I wearily replied and went back to reading my book.

Suddenly Mick shouted out, 'No! Don't!' I looked over my shoulder to see his face staring at the entrance to our tent with a look of sheer horror on his face. Then I clocked on to what he was looking at. It was Les's arse shoved through the flap of our tent. With that, Les said, 'Goodnight, lads!' and then cracked a huge, thunderous one off, that smelt like he'd been storing it up ever since his last curry.

'Foul bowel strikes again!' cried Les as he ran back to his tent, leaving us to deal with his vile aroma.

For some strange reason, Les and my other mates found this prank hysterical. Quickly, Mick and me exited the tent pretty sharpish as we were in desperate need of fresh air. The only positive in this episode was that at least Les was wearing boxer shorts. The revolting sight of his bare arse would have been appalling, something that would have been seared into my memory forever.

13

CHELSEA'S FIRST defeat of the season came at Derby thanks to a penalty in the 50th minute, scored by Steve Buckley. The first home game I went to was the 1-1 draw against Leicester where Tony McAndrew scored his first goal for the Blues.

By October it was becoming pretty clear that the much-hoped-for promotion challenge was fast disappearing over the horizon. One game that offered some brief light in a tunnel of darkness was at home to Grimsby. I was in two minds as to whether I would go as I'd had the flu all week and was still feeling the effects. And even though I'd had a few days off work, I decided that I'd recovered enough to take up yet again my usual place in front of the tea bar. In my early days at the Bridge, at 14 years of age, I was lacking somewhat in inches so I stood along with my friends on top of the white wall with the concourse running below us which gave us an uninterrupted view of the pitch. But now at the age of 27 and being 6ft 3in tall, I'd long since given up that vantage point. To make matters worse, as well as feeling the effects of the flu, the weather was damp and miserable. For this generation of Chelsea fans it's probably hard to believe that there were just over 10,000 brave souls there that day, and I should imagine that Grimsby's away support was minuscule, to say the least.

After twice leading, only to be pegged back on each occasion, the Blues then went on to hit quickfire goals through giant centre-half Micky Droy and midfielder John Bumstead. With just two minutes remaining, David Speedie scored his second of the afternoon to give Chelsea a 5-2 win. Speedie was proving to be an astute acquisition. His all-action, high-energy style coupled with raw aggression was something we hadn't seen at the Bridge since the legendary Ian Hutchinson had retired back in 1976. Bryan 'Pop' Robson, however, was finding life tough back in the old Second Division, a league made up with a mixture of journeyman players, youngsters on their way up, and once-bright stars now descending into obscurity. In fact, though Pop scored a few more goals for the Blues, his appearances diminished to practically zero as the season wore on.

Though that win had cheered me up no end, I still felt decidedly rough. However, the prospect of staying in on a Saturday night with my parents was a fate I refused to comprehend. In those days Saturday night was *the* night, and to be sitting at home was almost a confirmation that you were, in fact, a social outcast. So, manfully, I met up with my mates at a local pub back in Hemel Hempstead. Immediately I knew that I'd made a schoolboy error. The mixture of noise and smoke that effused the bar seemed magnified to the nth degree. After about an hour, I decided to call it a night and left my mates to enjoy the rest of their Saturday evening. I walked back into the town centre and tried to get a taxi without any luck, then after waiting for a bus for about half an hour, which again was a no-show, I thought to myself, sod it, I'll walk home. Though it was about two and a half miles back, that was nothing unusual back in the day for me and my mates who quite often walked to the pub so that nobody had the burden of being lumbered with the role of designated driver, and we were free to consume as many pints as we liked.

That's not to say that we sometimes didn't foolishly flout the rules. For instance, I can remember coming home from Tim's flat on my motorbike one night after we'd consumed a duty-free bottle of J&B whisky which we drank neat as, in our opinion, watering down Scotch was, to our way of thinking, a heinous sin. I have no recollection of that night apart from Tim and his wife, Tracy, trying to persuade me to stay but it seemed that my mind was made up and I duly departed on my hazardous journey, of which I have no recall whatsoever. The next thing I remember is waking up in my own bed the following morning with the hangover from hell. Looking back now, I must have been stark raving mad to have attempted that ride home but a mixture of whisky and macho bullshit was indeed an intoxicating concoction.

Meanwhile, back in October 1982 when I'd left the pub early, I'd walked about halfway home from the town centre when suddenly the heavens opened and I was caught in a torrential downpour. By the time I got home I looked like a drowned rat, and consequently the flu I'd been suffering from quickly turned into pleurisy which laid me low for the next couple of weeks. Still, at least it meant time off work; not such an enjoyable experience when you're actually ill, rather than pulling a sickie. So what a weird day: feeling rough, then watching the Blues hit five, followed by a wretched evening in the pub, and to top it all off, a complete drenching to round off proceedings.

* * *

Though Chelsea's form was patchy in the closing months of 1982, there was nothing to suggest that we'd be in danger of being relegated that season. Promotion, once again, seemed highly unlikely, and as our west London rivals QPR were looking more and more like strong candidates for the leap into the top division, things did look incredibly bleak. One highlight, however, was Colin Pates's piledriver against Charlton at the Bridge in late October, a tremendous 25-yard screamer that left visiting keeper Nicky Johns grasping at thin air. You can see that goal now on YouTube as the game was featured on ITV's *The Big Match.* I recently took a look at the footage and the goal still looks as good today as it did all that time ago. Chelsea won 3-1 with veteran striker Robson scoring the third goal in typical opportunistic fashion.

One thing I noticed from looking at the footage was how cheap and nasty football appeared in those days. The Bridge looked like it was slowly tumbling down and even our goal netting, which had always looked distinguished with the stanchions which always made the goals at the Bridge look really classy, were now replaced by netting that looked like it had been nicked from a Sunday league side playing on Hackney Marshes.

I will no doubt be accused of being a Luddite but I was no fan of the kits that were manufactured in those days. The shirts had become shinier, and the shorts were becoming shorter and shorter. As the seasons went by the size of the shorts became so small that they looked like nothing more than a pair of oversized Speedos. Having said all of that, the kits that Chelsea wore in between 1983 and 1985 have become all-time classics. I especially liked the all-yellow away strip with horizontal stripes on the shirt, the yellow shorts and the fantastic yellow socks with the blue and red hoops. Though in truth, the reason why that strip is so highly regarded today might have something to do with the fact that it was worn in such a successful period for the club. It seems as though I'm going to contradict myself because I've just remembered that the yellow away shirt we wore in the 1982/83 season, with a thin blue pinstripe, is also a bit of a classic. A couple of years ago I managed to buy one from eBay, with long sleeves. Those shirts are very hard to come by.

By the time Chelsea visited Carlisle United in mid-October, they had finally managed to get their man when they signed Joey Jones from Wrexham. Though some Blues fans weren't exactly thrilled when the Welshman signed, personally I was delighted. Though not blessed with great technical ability, Jones made up for that with a never-say-die spirit which ensured that he gave 100 per cent every time he stepped on to the pitch, something I felt Chelsea had been missing since the days of Chopper Harris and co. Jones's debut at Carlisle, however, didn't exactly go to plan when he was sent off in the second half of a 2-1 defeat. The story goes that he left the pitch to a chorus of boos from the home following and some of our away support. Not the greatest of starts but from then on, Jones became one of Chelsea's legendary cult heroes as his tough tackling and inspired leadership endeared him to the Stamford Bridge faithful.

Chelsea's form in the autumn of 1982 was as unpredictable as the weather. There was a depressing 1-0 defeat at Millmoor against Rotherham. What the hell was it about Rotherham? In the space of a year they'd beaten Chelsea three times and on each occasion the man in their dugout was the ever-grinning Emlyn Hughes. This was starting to become a nasty habit that we needed to stop as soon as possible. So when I went to Loftus Road to see us take on QPR, I was fearing the worst but yet again, in their infuriatingly quixotic way, Chelsea stunned the home crowd and the vast majority of their travelling support when they came back from a goal down to take all of the points with goals from Clive Walker and the increasingly impressive David Speedie.

While the Blues sat in 12th place after that win, the season would then gradually implode, leaving them standing on the brink of relegation to the old Third Division. Did I have any fear of the drop that day on the way home from Loftus Road? Not at all. I just figured that it would be yet another campaign of mid-table mediocrity, with the occasional highlight that I'd witnessed that day. Any hopes of another long run in the FA Cup to ease the pain of our poor league form were ended at Derby County. With memories of the previous season's run to the quarter-finals, I made my way to the Baseball Ground hoping and praying that we'd overcome our Second Division rivals to make it into the draw for the last 16. When Mike Fillery equalised for the Blues with just ten minutes left, it looked like a replay at the Bridge was on the cards. That was until Derby grabbed a last-minute winner. For some reason that defeat is still one that I remember to this day as being one of the lowest moments I've experienced following Chelsea.

While checking details for this book, I discovered that both of Derby's goals in their 2-1 win were scored by Kevin Wilson, who went on later to have a successful spell at the Bridge as part of the team that won the the Second Division title in 1988/89. I have to admit that throughout Wilson's career at the club and during the ensuing decades, I was totally unaware that the moustachioed striker was the main reason for my devastation at the horrible, cruel defeat we suffered that afternoon. Our chance for revenge came the following Saturday when Chelsea were due to play the same opponents at the Bridge. Sadly, the Blues failed to take their chance for revenge and went down to a dismal 3-1 defeat. They even managed to give the visitors a helping hand by scoring two own goals, the culprits being

Steve Francis and John Bumstead. Our best performance at home that season happened around the same time when we thrashed Cambridge United 6-0 at the Bridge. However, any celebration about the fact that we'd beaten the men from the Abbey Stadium by an aggregate score of 7-0 that season shows you just how far our expectations had plummeted.

14

THE MUSIC scene of the early 1980s was eclectic to say the least. I can remember the *NME* constantly remarking about the number of bands who had blond hair such as Bucks Fizz, Dollar, and many other lookalikes. It seemed that more and more bands were deciding that blond was best. One group in particular that I loathed was the execrable Japan, whose lead singer, David Sylvian, did his best David Bowie impersonation, which I found to be hugely embarrassing. Though my main interest at the time were acts like Elvis Costello and the Jam, I have to admit that I've always had a deep love of bubblegum pop. Back when I was a teenager, alongside my love for the Beatles, Bowie, Roxy Music, Lou Reed, and the Who, I have no problem in confessing that I was a fan of 'Love Grows Where My Rosemary Goes' by Edison Lighthouse. Fluff it may be, but as a piece of supremely crafted pop songwriting it's right up there. Another reason I've always loved that song is that I have a vividly clear memory of that being played at the Bridge during Pete Owen's pre-match spin, before the third-round FA Cup tie against Birmingham in January 1970 at the start of a cup run which, as we all know, would see us lift that trophy for the first time in our history.

Another huge piece of cheddar I really like was 'Beach Baby' by First Class, which was released in the summer of

1974. First Class weren't actually a working band at all, but a bunch of session musicians based in Hounslow, who somehow managed to fool the USA into believing that they were from San Francisco or LA by creating a pop masterpiece that still sounds as astounding today as it did back then. Interestingly, both of those songs had on lead vocals Tony Burrows who at that time was the go-to session singer. In fact, he's the only man to appear in an episode of *Top of the Pops* performing with three different groups, as part of Edison Lighthouse with 'Love Grows Where My Rosemary Goes', White Plains with 'My Baby Loves Loving', and the original Brotherhood of Man with 'United We Stand'.

I also have to confess to seeing Bucks Fizz live at the Dominion Theatre on Tottenham Court Road in early 1983. You might think that someone who'd seen Elvis Costello, David Bowie, the Who, Lou Reed, Squeeze and Ian Dury live would look down their nose at a manufactured pop group. And to be honest there was a feeling of what the hell are we doing but, because me, Mick and Pete were in London that day we all thought why not give it a go, and I have to say that they were bloody brilliant. Their vocals were great and the backing band were all high-class musos.

Pete, who'd been our drummer in the Intros, was and still is, a bloke who could charm the birds out of the trees. Just before Bucks Fizz were due to come on stage, I noticed that he was missing. Where the bloody hell has he got to, I thought. My question was answered when he suddenly appeared with three backstage passes to meet the Fizz. How he managed to swing that, God only knows. We quickly had a discussion on whether we should go behind the curtain but, thankfully, common sense prevailed. Seeing that the three of us were around 27 years of age, it would mean that we'd stick out like a sore thumb among all of the young kids in attendance there that night and we therefore declined the invitation. Though their breakthrough single, 'Making Your Mind Up', which was released in the summer of 1981 and also won the Eurovision Song Contest, was total bubblegum, they went on to have a string of hits that were beautifully crafted pop songs.

Another guilty pleasure I have to confess to are two Dollar singles, both produced by Trevor Horn, 'Hand Held in Black and White' and 'Give Me Back My Heart'. Though the charts were often full of dross with the occasional gem, today's sorry state of the charts makes the 1980s now seem, in retrospect, a golden era. Though in my opinion, the 1960s will never be beaten for the amazingly high standard of killer singles. A close second is the 1970s, albeit in two different phases – the early part of the decade with the breakthrough of Davie Bowie, Roxy Music, Sparks, and Cockney Rebel, and the latter years when punk and new wave gave us all hope that we were entering a bright new era, only for disco to raise its ugly head and completely engulf the charts.

* * *

Alongside Chelsea's misfortunes on the pitch, the spring of 1983 is a time that holds bittersweet memories for me. Back in the autumn of 1982 we had taken on two female singers to join the band. I finally had to realise that my voice, though passable for live work, was cruelly exposed in the studio. This was made brutally clear to me by a horrible old hippie called Paul Brett. He'd previously been in the Strawbs and various other well-known bands. He'd also had an album that had charted back in 1980, titled *Romantic Guitar*. I think you can guess from this title that this would be a record which would never find itself on my turntable. Brett was a brilliant guitar player and didn't he let you know it. The original plan was that I'd do the vocals on the two tracks that we were recording but it soon became evident that Brett didn't rate me as a vocalist in any way, shape or form, and to my horror the other people in the studio seemed to agree with him. So having very little choice, I handed over the vocals to Brett himself. Though his voice was nothing to write home about, he knew how to use a studio and he even sang harmonies. Looking back, though it was hard to take, Brett taught me a valuable lesson that day: stick to songwriting and playing the guitar. And since that excruciating setback, I've never returned to the microphone as a singer.

At the beginning of 1983, me and Dave, our keyboard player, went to London armed with our demo tape that we'd recorded with our two new female singers. It's hard to believe in this day and age that we actually went round to different record companies, and basically just knocked on their doors. It was a really miserable experience and the gloomy January weather, coupled with a bone-chilling wind, was hardly helped by the the curt rebuffs we got that day. I think a couple of them took some of our tapes but nothing ever came of it. Although, having said that, we did manage to get to see an A&R man at some little indie label, but all he did was give us a stream of bullshit about all the people he knew in the industry, while our tape was playing in the background. It was blatantly obvious that he wasn't even listening to our efforts. However, he did have one final insult that was pointed in our direction as we left his shabby little office.

'It's not bad, boys. But you've got a long way to go.'

Soaked and disenchanted, we caught the train home and for the next few days I did nothing but sulk and wondered if this was worth carrying on with. This is the point where loads of musicians throw the towel in. Thankfully, I steadied myself and vowed that I was not going to take any notice of what that idiot had said. Even though I could have wallpapered my room with rejection slips, no, I thought – be positive! So later in the week I sent a tape in to *Melody Maker*, which had a feature where they reviewed demos from new acts. Why not, I thought. I've got nothing to lose, well, apart from my sanity and my fast disappearing sense of pride. With that I totally forgot about the tape as the weeks went by. I did occasionally look to see if our tape had been reviewed, but with no luck. Then in late March, I was eating my breakfast and getting ready for work when I picked up *Melody Maker*, which I had delivered every week. While I was eating my cornflakes, I started reading the demo section when to my amazement I saw that our tape had been reviewed. I almost spat out my cereals as I told my dad, 'Bloody hell! We've got a review!'

Quickly I read what the journalist had written. It was, indeed, a great review, even quoting lyrics I had written to one of the tracks. He also likened the guitar riff that I'd played on one of the songs to 'Remote Control' by the Clash. Our contact details were shown at the end of the review and when I got in from work that evening I saw a note my dad had left me which contained the names of all the record companies that had phoned that day, including RCA, EMI, Island Records and Chrysalis. There were also some calls from some indie labels. Unbelievably, one of them was from that smug A&R man who'd told us a few weeks earlier that we still had a long way to go. He'd obviously totally forgotten us, such was the lack of interest he'd shown in our music. This was my first experience of the power of the written word. Somebody in the music business had endorsed us and now the doors that had been firmly shut in our faces for so long were suddenly opening.

Through this review I was able to experience the world of recording and publishing that I'd only ever dreamed about, and though our band line-up at the time was not the one eventually signed to an indie label, I at least now had my foot in the door. I also have to thank DJ Charlie Gillett and producer Pat Collier, who both championed my cause and were both instrumental in my signing my first recording contract.

On the night that we'd received the review, me and Dave went out and got very drunk. Life at that moment was great. We had record companies chasing us. What could go wrong, I thought. Sadly, I was then to see how life can turn on the spin of a coin when me and my mates got a call to let us know that another one of our friends, Dave Hyde, had terminal leukaemia. In your mid-20s you're under the illusion that you're invincible, so to get the news that somebody you'd known since we were all boys was going to die was a terrible awakening to the fragility of life. Me and Mick made a journey down to the hospital in Bath where Dave was receiving treatment. In true English stoicism, no one mentioned what was now inevitable. It was a tough day. I can remember going for a walk in the hospital grounds and seeing two nurses playing tennis on their day off. The weather was beautiful and it must be said that this was an idyllic scene that seemed to say, and so the world turns. Saying goodbye to Dave for what we knew would be the last time is a memory that still remains vivid to this day.

On 23 April 1983, Dave passed away. He was just 28 years old. That such a force of nature could be struck down like that at such a tender age was devastating. I'd know Dave since I was 14 years old. We'd played football together, we'd gone on holidays together, and though we'd known of his illness during the last couple of years, whenever we asked him how he was doing, he always said,

'I'm fine, no problem.' I found out that he'd passed away when I was in a studio recording some new songs. When I heard that JD, another one of my mates, was on the phone for me, I knew what was coming. So in the space of a few weeks I'd seen both sides of the coin: elation at the interest from record companies, followed by the tragic passing of one of my best mates.

I can remember that afternoon at the hospital when we were visiting Dave, of going to the TV room to find out how Chelsea had got on. Not well, as it turned out. They'd lost 2-0 at home to Newcastle. It was now becoming apparent that the Blues were in serious trouble, and the threat of relegation to the Third Division was becoming a real possibility, though that afternoon, visiting Dave in the hospital for the final time, football didn't really matter much at all. Bill Shankly's much-reported quote that 'football is not a matter of life and death, it's more important than that', while funny, is in effect, as I learned that day in that hospital in Bath, complete and utter rubbish.

* * *

Around that time I started going out with one of our girl singers, Clare, a relationship that should never have lasted the long three and a half years that it did. I think both of us knew that this was an affair that had a date stamp on it. But for my part I took the cowardly way out, that it's better to be in a misfiring couple than to be thrown back into the lonely world of being single. She was from an upper-middle-class background, whereas I was from a working-class family. I discovered fairly quickly that I despised the circle of friends she had, who were the embodiment of that new breed called the Yuppie. God knows how many times I was asked what my career ambitions were, or how many Ks I hoped to earn. Much to Clare's horror, this type of questioning brought out a heightened, laddish version of myself, and before too long, I was acting out the part of the Chelsea-supporting, music-loving Jack-the-Lad.

None of her crowd were drinkers, whereas me and my mates were not averse to more than a few bevvies, which led to some embarrassing incidents including at one party, where I was trying to demonstrate how big Joe McLaughlin, the Chelsea centre-back, headed the ball away by purposely smashing my head into a 'For Sale' sign outside the flat next door. Thank God the sign was made out of very thin wood, and wasn't one of those metal ones. Then there was a time when one of Clare's girlfriends was asking me about how I was enjoying work. I didn't have the heart to tell her that I was doing my level best to avoid it, let alone enjoy it. I was at that time a little bit worse for wear through my consumption of one too many whiskies, which was the cause of me tipping the chilli con carne and the jacket potato off my plate, straight down her top.

'Now look what you've done!' shouted Clare.

Oh, dear, I thought. This is not going to go down well. To make matters worse, I then decided in my drunken stupor to wipe away the chunks of food which had engulfed her top. In retrospect, perhaps not the best of moves.

In May 1984 I took Clare to see her first game of football. It was the Blues' home fixture against Barnsley. It was a vital game, more of which I will go into later on, but taking her was a poor decision all round. She looked bored shitless for the whole 90 minutes and was appalled at the riff-raff surrounding her in front of the tea bar. She finally put the icing on the cake when she cheered Barnsley's equaliser, a goal that was met by deathly silence by everyone around us. Yet again I was met with withering looks from the Chelsea fans around me, similar to ones I'd received back in December 1976 when my previous girlfriend, Vicky, asked how many balls they play with when the game kicks off. Thankfully, that day against Barnsley turned out well in the end as Chelsea added two more goals to run out 3-1 winners. If I had to give advice to anyone who is having any doubts about their relationship, I would strongly suggest to try living together, which is without doubt the acid test. All the foibles and irritating habits are magnified ten-fold. Those ten months we lived together were some of the most miserable of my life. We'd only been living in the flat for a couple of months when I realised that we'd both made a terrible mistake.

One Saturday in March 1986, I was due to go to the home game against West Ham. So keen was I to get out of the flat that I caught the 10am train to Euston, for a 3pm kick-off. Chelsea didn't exactly help lift me out of my black mood by getting turned over 4-0. It was a horrible, damp, dismal day in more ways than one. I can remember hanging about Kings Road that evening, not wanting to go back to Clare and what was, after all, supposed to be home. Consequently I decided to find a pub. So, finally, this is what it had come to. I was now the solitary bloke, nursing a pint of beer, something I'd seen on countless occasions, but had never imagined that one day this would also be my fate.

Going back in time to January 1985, another incident occurred that showed Clare's lack of understanding of what it was to support Chelsea. On the night of that legendary 4-4 draw with Sheffield Wednesday at Hillsborough in the League Cup quarter-final replay, I was due to meet her for a drink. I'd been to the first game at the Bridge, which had ended in a 1-1 draw with Kerry Dixon, yet again, missing from the penalty spot. In those days there were no penalty shoot-outs so consequently that meant a replay up in Sheffield. I can remember having the radio on in my music room as goal after goal went past Eddie Niedzwiecki. With the Blues 3-0 down at half-time, like every other Chelsea fan, I thought that was it. The comeback in the second half by the yellow-shirted team has been frequently heralded as one of the club's most iconic nights and, unbelievably, Chelsea led 4-3 through two goals by Paul Canoville, with Kerry Dixon and Micky Thomas also hitting the net. With just a few minutes to go and already half an hour late for my date that evening, I was caught between a rock and a hard place. Then the phone rang with Clare asking me where I'd got to.

'I'm just leaving now,' I lied, not revealing the reason for my poor timekeeping.

Then I had an idea. I'd listen to the closing stages on my Walkman which would be no easy task because in those days, I had a motorbike which would have meant me stopping every few yards, to take off my helmet, put on the headphones and find out how the Blues were doing. There were just minutes left at Hillsborough as I made my way to my garage to get my motorbike. Surely, this was it. Somehow Chelsea had turned round what had looked like a lost cause into one of their most incredible achievements. I was just opening the garage door when Doug Rougvie intervened and literally stuck his foot in as he conceded a penalty. There's no doubt that it was a penalty. This was confirmed when I watched the highlights that night. It was, indeed, a sickening blow to be 3-0 down, then to lead 4-3 with seconds remaining and a place in the semi-finals within our grasp, leaving myself and every other Chelsea fan heartbroken. It also left me in a quandary of what the hell was I going to do. I couldn't fit the headphones under my crash helmet, which left me only one choice. I'd ride part of the way to Clare's house, stop the motorbike, put on the headphones and get an update. That 15-minute journey seemed to go on forever. Halfway there, I listened in to find out that the scores were still level at 4-4 and the game had gone into extra time. When I got to Clare's house, I rushed up to her bedroom where, would you believe, she was still getting ready. Instantly, I told her of my nightmarish predicament and that I wasn't leaving for a drink until the game had finished.

'How long is there to go?' she asked.

'About ten minutes,' I replied while trying to listen to the live commentary on my Walkman.

'Can't you just find out the score tomorrow?' she insanely enquired.

'No, I bloody can't. Have you gone mad?'

During all of this, she just sat there in front of her bedroom mirror, fixing her makeup and hair while I was suffering pitiless agony, as Sheffield Wednesday, boosted by their late reprieve, had Chelsea on the rack. I can clearly recall Wednesday striker Lee Chapman blasting over a close-range shot in the dying minutes. Almost immediately, the final whistle blew on an incredible night which has gone down as one of the most classic games in Chelsea's history.

Suddenly, I had a craving for a drink. I was emotionally drained. I don't remember much about that evening in the pub as my mind was on getting back to watch the highlights on *Sportsnight*. And what a brilliant game it was. The substitution at half-time in bringing young Paul Canoville on by manager John Neal paid off 12 seconds after the restart when he ran on to Dixon's flicked header to bring Chelsea back into the game. My other abiding memory is the look of bewilderment on Rougvie's face after he clumsily brought down a Wednesday player to concede the late penalty. He looked just like a kid who'd been caught out misbehaving, and was glancing round to see if he'd got away with it. Unfortunately, for poor old Doug, Mel Sterland, the boulder-headed caveman lookalike, duly despatched the penalty to rescue a draw for Wednesday that, on the balance of the game, they hardly deserved.

After the highlights had finished, Harry Carpenter, who was more known for his boxing commentary, announced that Chelsea had won the toss of the coin to stage the second replay at the Bridge, which softened the blow of conceding that late penalty. I went to that game on a freezing cold night and after falling behind, yet again, Chelsea levelled when David Speedie's header cancelled out Wednesday's opener. In reality, most of the plaudits for that goal must go down to a sublime piece of individuality and skill by the mercurial Pat Nevin. The game was still locked at 1-1 as it moved into the last minute when Chelsea were awarded a corner. As the ball was driven in by Canoville, little Micky Thomas darted in to send a flying header into the Wednesday net. With barely any time left, Wednesday knew that the game was up and a few minutes later, the referee blew for full time. Chelsea were through to the semi-final.

One thing I've noticed when watching that game back on YouTube is Nevin being kicked in the shins by a Wednesday defender as he tried to celebrate the winning goal. Poor little Pat fell to the ground like a sack of potatoes, but at that moment I should imagine that he was in such a state of euphoria he hardly noticed the loutish attempt at retribution. It was a pathetic challenge from a man who knew that he was beaten. So, all in all, Pat, and Chelsea, had the last laugh.

Those three games against Wednesday have gone down in Chelsea folklore. Personally, I couldn't stand Sheffield Wednesday and their taciturn manager, Howard Wilkinson. While Chelsea were a quicksilver team, Wednesday, in my opinion, were the embodiment of what was wrong in British football. They were all giants who battered not only their opponents, but also the ball, into submission. The running joke at the time was that as well as the opposing players being carried off at various times, the ball was also carried off on a stretcher after being battered from one end of the pitch to the other, such was Wednesday's reputation for being one of the prime culprits of the long-ball game.

* * *

Those ten months of purgatory I spent living with Clare came to an end in October 1986, and though it was hard to go back to being single, there's no doubt that it was the best thing for both of us. So many people from earlier generations who were brought up with a more stoic outlook of sticking together through thick and thin often ended up in marriages where both parties lived out their lives in quiet desperation. Two events that didn't help matters occurred just before the inevitable split, the first being when Clare invited her female boss and her boyfriend round for a meal. Her boss was the epitome of the Yuppie breed, all padded shoulders and carefully coiffured hair that never moved an inch out of place. The boyfriend, however, was a bit dodgy to say the least, and was what is commonly known as her bit of rough. There was a bit of silence at the dinner table when said boyfriend casually announced to Clare and myself that he'd been in trouble with the law for stealing cars. Clare's boss looked furious with him. It was a fact that she had had no intention of sharing with anyone, let alone the two of us. He then went on to blithely expand on his trials and tribulations with the police. Clare's boss then turned the subject back on to her favourite topic – work – and how much money she was earning. Clare was part of her sales team, and doing very nicely, thank you very much, with a good salary, foreign holidays and cases of champagne thrown in. On and on she went with endless invective of targets reached and how many thousands she was earning each year – a stupid lecture on what she called her 'career'. She then made the fatal mistake of asking me how my own career was going.

'OK,' I replied. 'I get up, go to work, then spend the rest of the day counting down the hours until I can go home,' which was not strictly true because at the time, I was working at Scammell Motors in Watford as a production controller, and, looking back, it was one of the best jobs I ever had, but at that precise moment I was in the mood to burst her precious bubble. Then she left me with an open goal when she announced that she'd often thought about going into medicine. My God, I thought, she's handing this to me on a plate.

'Have you considered brain surgery?' I asked.

'In what aspect are you talking about?'

'Having it!' I replied.

For a moment there was a deafening silence that was broken by her dodgy date for the evening who burst out laughing and slapped the table with both hands.

'Nice one, mate. I like that,' he chuckled.

Unfortunately, Clare's boss didn't see the funny side of the comment and looked absolutely furious. That's the trouble with people like that. They're so full of their own self-importance that they seem to suffer from a humour bypass. Clare gave me a withering look which I totally ignored. We'd barely finished our dessert when Clare's boss brought out her Filofax, and, after a brief look, said, 'Actually, I've got an early meeting tomorrow. We'd better make a move.'

'I'll get your coat,' I replied, vowing that this would be the last time that I'd ever be in her company.

After Clare had shown her to the door and said goodnight, she came into the kitchen where I was starting to do the washing up, and snapped, 'You just had to, didn't you?'

'I'm sorry, I have no idea what you are talking about,' I replied – a remark that added more fuel to the fire.

'Yes, you do. That remark about brain surgery,' Clare said.

'Well,' I replied, 'she's a total bore who does nothing but talk about herself and her poxy job.'

Then I decided to throw in a literary quote just to show what a smartarse I was.

'As Oscar Wilde once quipped,' I said while putting on the most pompous voice I could affect, '"Falling in love with yourself is usually a lifelong affair."'

Clare, not exactly being the literary type, looked bemused as my intended barb went sailing over her head and right out of the window.

The second incident was that Clare, who'd been singing in our project for nearly four years, had been coming in for criticism from the other members. They argued that her voice wasn't versatile enough and couldn't cope with the harder, edgier material, and therefore we were condemned as writers to just turn out ballads and soft, melodic pop. In truth, I could see their point. I knew that she was struggling and while the rest of us were desperate to get a record deal, she saw the project as just a nice hobby. For months I had people in my ear telling me that she'd got to go. Their protests were further strengthened when an A&R person at EMI said we would need to find a new singer as she was detracting from the music. Keyboard player Dave, who wasn't exactly subtle, said that we needed a singer with a bit of an edge. He then went on brutally to say, 'Look, to me, it sounds that the feeling and passion she projects in our songs, is like someone sitting in a bath of cold water.' It really was a terrible situation. Did I allow nepotism to rear its ugly head because she was my girlfriend, who I just happened to be living with? Or should I do the professional thing and tell her, like I would anyone else, that things musically weren't working out and that we needed to make a change? For days I agonised over my decision. It didn't help matters when I kept on getting phone calls from the other members from the band saying, 'Have you told her yet?'

Left with no choice, as I was determined to have a career in the music business, I bit the bullet and told her that the band, including myself, wanted to try something new and that we were going to advertise for two new girl singers who could handle the power pop we intended to write, and who would be up for handling live work. This was something that Clare had made patently clear she had no intention of ever doing. I know it seems hard, and you might say that I was callous, but later on when we got a record deal, I learned very quickly just how cut-throat the music business can be.

By the beginning of 1987 we had two new girl singers, one of whom was Trudie, who would later on become my girlfriend and we're still together to this day. When we signed to an indie label, I was shocked at how much pressure was put on the female singer fronting a band. Whereas Clare would have folded like a pack of cards, Trudie, though she found the scrutiny tough to take, managed to get through it and had a brilliant voice, whether in the studio or on stage.

15

ON 5 March 1983, I went to see Chelsea play Charlton at The Valley, a ground that didn't exactly have pleasant memories for me. In 1974, I'd gone to see the Who play there alongside 80,000 other people. While the bands that day were great, the handling of that vast crowd left a lot to be desired. From midday until the Who finished their performance at about 11pm, we'd all stood there for all those hours without food or drink. And as for the toilet facilities, if they existed at all, we then had to contend with the boiling hot weather, but back in those days, apparently, dehydration and heatstroke was not something that caused any cause for concern with the organisers of that fiasco.

Then of course there was that horrible game at The Valley during the 1976/77 promotion season when we'd been well and truly turned over 4-0 by the home side. Now, in 1983, it seemed that the curse of The Valley was rearing its ugly head once again as Charlton took a two-goal lead. Somehow though, the Blues rallied and managed to level at 2-2. The first of the goals was scored by Pop Robson, in what turned out to be his last goal and last appearance for the Blues. Surely we'd take the initiative as the home side looked shell-shocked at Chelsea's unlikely comeback. Even though there was still half an hour to play, in all honesty, I would have taken a point. After all, beggars can't be choosers. Sadly my hopes were obliterated when Charlton scored three times in less than ten minutes. We even gave them a helping hand when Colin Pates put through his own net to restore the home team's advantage. In the next few minutes, the Blues descended into a shambles as Charlton hit two quickfire goals to take an unassailable 5-2 lead. With still 20 minutes to play I feared the worst, that we'd be on the wrong end of a cricket score, and though Charlton smelled blood, neither side added to their tally. All of Chelsea's frailties and shortcomings were cruelly exposed that day as, yet again, we all embarked on the depressing journey back to Victoria on the old bone-shaker that passed for a train.

I can then recall that awful 3-0 drubbing handed out by Barnsley at the Bridge as one of the most depressing afternoons I'd ever spent in front of the tea bar. Once again, we gave them a helping hand when the unfortunate Kevin Hales put through his own goal. This was a habit we needed to break as soon as possible. You'd think that after that humbling result, the visit to promotion-chasing Fulham the following week would be a nailed-on home banker. But, yet again, Chelsea upset the form book by gaining a valuable 1-1 draw after Paul Canoville volleyed the Blues ahead. We'd hardly had time to celebrate before the home side equalised through Kevin Lock. Still, it was a point, a very valuable one as it turned out. Those dropped points by Fulham would in some way be responsible for them missing out on promotion during the last few weeks of a season which, in all honesty, is hard to write about.

After the awful 3-0 humiliation against Burnley at Turf Moor on 23 April, we then had two consecutive home games over the bank holiday. Win them and we were virtually safe, but those hopes came back to bite us hard when first of all we drew 1-1 against bogey team Rotherham. I never realised when I started writing this book just how much we used to struggle against that lot. Our next crack at salvation came two days later at the Bridge against Sheffield Wednesday. But after taking a first-half lead through David Speedie, we sat back. We spent most of the second half trying to defend that precious advantage which resulted in us handing back the initiative to Wednesday, who attacked us constantly. There was a sickening predictability when the visitors levelled in the 67th minute through Gary Bannister. Typically, as so often happens when a team are pegged back, the Blues then went in search of a winner. Despite our best efforts, unfortunately there was to be no salvation as the game ended in a 1-1 draw. If I remember correctly, it was a dark, wet, miserable bank holiday Monday, weather that seemed to sum up Chelsea's fortunes at that moment.

Now it was clear that it was a four-way fight to beat the drop with Rotherham, Burnley and Bolton joining Chelsea in what would be a battle to the bitter end. That meant that the following Saturday's trip to Burnden Park to face Bolton on 7 May would virtually be a relegation decider. How had it come to this? How had the club I'd followed since 1967 fallen so far from grace? But these were the facts we had to face. We had to get something from Bolton to have any chance of maintaining our Second Division status.

Yet again there was a week of psychological torture. Moments of hope were swiftly followed by black clouds of doubt. The prospect of seeing Chelsea plying their trade in the Third Division was, in a word, unthinkable. I couldn't get to the Bolton game so once again, I would be listening to the radio for news, and seeing that a relegation clash in the Second Division would hardly be at the top of the agenda for broadcasters, I was painfully aware that the updates would be few and far between. I sat in my music room at home, knowing that I was going to endure 90 minutes of torture. I even made various trips downstairs, and to the loo, conning myself that nothing could happen when my back was turned, and at half-time the score was Bolton 0 Chelsea 0. Right then, I would have taken a point which would have meant that we'd have to beat Middlesbrough in the final home game of the season to ensure safety for another year. At last, around half past five, I was shaken out of my reverie by the radio announcer saying those ominous words, 'There's been a goal at Burnden Park.'

Instantly, my stomach fell to the floor. What had gone on? Those few seconds of waiting seemed like an eternity until finally I heard that Clive Walker had just scored the goal that the commentator said would 'surely keep Chelsea up'. I was ecstatic. I then found myself in fugue state, not knowing what I was going to do for the last 18 minutes. For what seemed a lifetime I paced around the music room, then on to the landing, all the time dreading another update. And then my nerves really kicked in and I resorted to my old habit of rushing to the loo to throw up. Two visits were paid on this occasion. The waiting was agonising but finally I heard the news that every Chelsea supporter had been praying for in a match which turned out to be one of the most vital wins in the club's history. Walker's priceless strike had put our fate into our own hands. A point against Middlesbrough would ensure that we stayed up, condemning Rotherham, Bolton and Burnley to the Third Division.

* * *

On 14 May in front of a near-20,000 crowd, Chelsea played out a dour, goalless draw with Middlesbrough at the Bridge to earn the point that confirmed we'd saved our Second Division status. The reaction from the Blues fans there that day was a mixture of celebration and relief that the club had saved themselves by the skin of their teeth. That win against Bolton had been invaluable. I've seen photographs of that game, which was played out on a pitch that was saturated. There's a great photo of Walker hitting the winner, and another brilliant image of the yellow-shirted Chelsea players throwing their tops to the away support.

The story goes that so hard-up were the club that chairman Ken Bates docked the price of those discarded shirts out of the players' wages the following week. Another story is that when Walker's shot hit the back of the net, several players who were now on the periphery of the first team sat motionless with barely a flicker of emotion as the final whistle went, unlike the suspended David Speedie who celebrated wildly, which showed that he for one had commitment and passion for the club, something he would display over the coming seasons.

A few days after the dust had settled, I, like many other Chelsea fans, wondered just what the future would hold for our club. An 18th-place finish in the Second Division was just not good enough for a club of this size. Don't get me wrong, no one has a divine right in the world of football to expect success just because they've achieved great things in the past. Yes, Spurs. You know who I'm talking about. Surely things had to change. Little did we know of the seismic plans that Bates and manager John Neal were plotting that summer, events which would lead to a sea change of some magnitude taking place at the Bridge.

Within weeks there was an exodus of players who Mr Bates referred to as 'dead wood' heading for the exit door, as the playing staff was ruthlessly culled. The likes of Alan Mayes, Gary Chivers, Gary Locke and Phil Driver were told that their services were no longer required in what was Chelsea's very own version of the 'Night of the Long Knives'. Trouble was, not being a club rolling in money, how were we going to recruit new players with money being so tight? We didn't have long to wait over that summer, which proved to be one of the most fruitful and exciting times in the club's history, when names including Kerry Dixon, Pat Nevin, Nigel Spackman and Joe McLaughlin all arrived at the Bridge. And to top that off, Chelsea also signed keeper Eddie Niedzwiecki from Wrexham. Those acquisitions were an inspired piece of business. Though the players were largely unknown, they were all young and hungry for success. Added to this influx was two members of the 1970 FA Cup winning-team – John Hollins, who would be player-coach, and the mercurial Alan Hudson, who had left the Bridge under a cloud back in 1974. Though Hollins was 37 years old, he was still as fit as a fiddle. As well as his off-field duties he would go on to play a substantial role in the first team for the coming season. Unfortunately for Huddy, things never worked out during his second spell and he departed back to his former club, Stoke, midway through the season.

I can remember the day that Kerry Dixon signed for the Blues from Fourth Division champions Reading. The fee of £175,000 was a bit of a gamble. It was a lot of money for a player who'd only ever appeared in the lowest tier of the Football League. Still, his goalscoring record for Reading in their promotion season had been excellent, and seeing that a host of First Division clubs had been interested in him, it was, without doubt, a bit of a coup, and would turn out to be one of the club's most astute signings. I was working in Watford in the summer of 1983 and used to go to a park every lunchtime to have my sandwiches and read the paper. That summer was a really hot one, and I can clearly recall sitting on a grass bank with the sun beating down as I overheard the transistor radio of someone who was sunbathing nearby. It announced that Chelsea had completed the signing of Dixon. Bloody hell, I thought, old Batesy is really splashing the cash.

That summer was almost like Christmas morning when you were a kid opening your presents, as one player after another seemed to be arriving at the Bridge on a weekly basis. I remember reading in the paper one day that Chelsea had signed the 19-year-old Clyde winger Pat Nevin for £95,000, which I thought was a bit steep for a teenager who, at that time, many people – including myself – had never heard of. That shows you just how wrong you can be, as wee Pat went on to become one of the most iconic players ever to wear the royal blue shirt of Chelsea.

* * *

As I made my way to the Bridge on Saturday, 27 August 1983 on what was another glorious summer afternoon, my feelings were mixed. How would the new players gel together, four of whom would be making their debuts? Our opponents were Derby County, who were managed at the time by Brian Clough's old sidekick, Peter Taylor. The bookies had made Derby one of the favourites for promotion, while Chelsea were seen as nothing more than a mid-table bet at best owing to our flirtation with relegation during the previous season. Yet again I took up my favourite position just in front of the tea bar, the same place I'd been standing in since my first solo visit to the Bridge in February 1969, when at 14 years of age I'd seen Chelsea destroy Sunderland 5-1 with my hero, Bobby Tambling, hitting four of the goals. That afternoon against Derby was the first time I'd set eyes on the new home strip with the horizontal red and white stripes on the classic royal blue shirts.

One player missing from the line-up that day was the stylish midfielder Mike Fillery, who Chelsea wanted to keep hold of during the big clear-out back in May. But Fillery's head was not for turning and he decided to leave what he felt was a sinking ship to join QPR, a decision which, at the time, must have seemed to have been a move in the right direction but ended up as nothing more than a fast-track into obscurity.

Four minutes of the new season had elapsed when part of our new-look midfield, Nigel Spackman, fired Chelsea ahead. For the rest of the first half the home side dominated the visitors but at half-time still only led by that early Spackman strike. The second half, however, was a different matter. Instead of losing our way like we had done on countless occasions the previous season when we had taken a lead, Chelsea doubled their advantage through Clive Walker. We'd barely stopped celebrating that goal when full-back Chris Hutchings added a third. Chelsea were totally wiping the floor with Derby and a perfect day got even better when Kerry Dixon hit his first two goals for the Blues, the second of which came with still over 20 minutes to play. I think if the referee had said to Peter Taylor, 'Do you want to throw the towel in?' he would have bitten his hand off. Derby looked tired and dispirited and were fortunate that Chelsea took their foot off the pedal while still controlling the game, and no further goals were added. In my wildest dreams, I could never have imagined the final score of Chelsea 5 Derby 0.

This new Chelsea side were unrecognisable from the previous season. To top it all off, we'd thrashed a team who'd beaten us three times during the last campaign. It was such a lovely day that I walked all the way back to Victoria so that I could do a bit of window-shopping down Kings Road. On the way I stopped off at a book shop, searching yet again for something new to read. I then noticed the bloke standing next to me, and here's one for the kids, he was the host of TV's *University Challenge*, Bamber Gascoigne, whose presenting style was far more urbane than the acerbic Jeremy Paxman, who replaced him in the role. I was tempted to ask him for 'a starter for ten' but decided, wisely, to let that one slide.

Though the whole team had played well against Derby, I can remember being really impressed by the 37-year-old player-coach John Hollins. Incredibly, he didn't look a day older than when he was part of the great cup-winning Chelsea side of the early 1970s. He still had the same boundless energy and was a wise head among so many young players. Though I was delighted with the performance against Derby, I wasn't going to get carried away. As the saying goes, 'One swallow doesn't make a summer.' But at least it was a more than positive start, and who knows, we hoped, the pundits might be wrong. Perhaps we could be considered seriously as one of the promotion hopefuls?

Next up was a trip to Brighton. I went to this game with a horrible piece of work who, looking back, had been one of the first cases of those money-grabbing idiots who pervaded the 1980s – the Yuppie. He'd got tickets for the stands, and though he talked incessantly on the journey down there about how much he was earning, I just kept my lip buttoned and let him prattle on. The thing was that he didn't even support Brighton or Chelsea, and as far as I could make out he knew very little about football. It was just one of those weird one-off things that you can experience going to games: a solitary encounter with someone who you will never see again. I seem to remember that it was through my new girlfriend, Clare, that I got to know him. Apparently he was trying his luck with one of her mates. As far as I know, he got precisely nowhere in his romantic quest. It just shows you how much of an impact he made on me at the Goldstone Ground that I have no clue of what his name was. It seems that while my memory is really good, it is also rather selective as the unfortunate character's identity has been consigned to the deepest, darkest recesses of my brain, labelled 'not worth thinking about'.

That day at Brighton, which was another sunny, late-summer afternoon, was packed with Chelsea away support. Indeed, it looked like the whole of Stamford Bridge had decided to invade that genteel seaside town. Brighton's home following was so heavily outnumbered that there appeared to be support for the Blues from all four sides of the ground. This was also the first time I got to see the iconic yellow away strip, the one with the blue and red horizontal stripes, with yellow shorts and those brilliant yellow socks with the blue and red hoops. The Brighton supporters next to us seemed intimidated at backing their side.

After Dixon put us ahead from the penalty spot, we looked to be on our way and that's the way it stayed until, with just 14 minutes left, Brighton equalised. I'm in no doubt that we'd have lost that game the previous season. But this was a very different Chelsea side and, within five minutes, Dixon struck again and that's the way it stayed until full time, with Chelsea recording an impressive 2-1 win.

Brighton had been relegated the previous season and had also reached the FA Cup Final where they'd lost to Manchester United in a replay at Wembley, a second attempt that United were fortunate to get after Gordon Smith fluffed an easy chance with only Gary Bailey to beat. Somehow the striker allowed Bailey to smother the ball with the scores locked at 2-2 in extra time. Brighton's fleeting chance had been and gone, so they inevitably went on to surrender meekly, 4-0 in the replay. Still, this team contained some seasoned pros like Jimmy Case, Tony Grealish, and Smith, so for Chelsea to come away that day with all the points was no mean feat.

The one disappointment was that just before the final whistle, Paul Canoville was sent off, which was followed by a pitch invasion. This event caused a storm in the media the following day with the same old hackneyed platitudes being given another airing, such as 'Chelsea hordes cause seaside terror'. Another headline was simply 'Chelsea's shame!' I don't know what it is but to this day, any form of supposed indiscretion committed by Chelsea Football Club is pounced upon by the press, like piranhas in the middle of a feeding frenzy. There were even reports that the Chelsea players had incited the violence by giving a clenched-fist salute to the massive away support. The ringleader of this post-match practice was usually Joey Jones, who in fact had been an unused substitute. This ritual was seen many times over the coming months and I and thousands of Blues fans loved it. At long last, we had a team who cared as much as we did about the club. The swagger and style that we'd last seen in the 1976/77 promotion season, had returned, and with it, a sense of pride and hope was endemic in everyone who had a special place in their heart for Chelsea.

* * *

One thing I was determined to do was to buy that brilliant yellow away shirt at the next home game, against Cambridge United, which Chelsea won 2-1, and I headed straight to the club shop after the final whistle. Despite going a goal down early on, Chelsea had rallied and gone on to take all the points on a wet and blustery afternoon through goals by John Bumstead and Clive Walker, who grabbed the winner with just 14 minutes left. This win put us second in the table, a position that we could only have dreamed about over the previous season. For once Kerry Dixon failed to score, a hiccup in form that was remedied the following Wednesday night when he scored all the goals in a 4-0 win over Gillingham in the League Cup at the Bridge to send the Blues through to the next round.

That night was the first time that I'd seen Pat Nevin, and though he would go on to become one of the club's most beloved players, as far as I can remember his debut was a quiet one. Nevin wrote in his autobiography, *The Accidental Footballer*, that there was a collective groan around the Bridge when he failed to control the ball on what would have been his first touch for the club. To be honest, I can't remember that, and I'm sure that all of us would have forgiven that mistake as Pat more than made up for this error during his time with the Blues.

Next up was a trip to Sheffield Wednesday, who were also among the early pace-setters in the Second Division. Despite going in front at Hillsborough in the second minute through Clive Walker with a goal where, if I remember correctly, he found himself to be the only player in Wednesday's half, Chelsea failed to capitalise on their lead and, sure enough, Wednesday equalised. It looked as though the game was heading for a 1-1 draw which would have been a really creditable result against one of our closest rivals. Unfortunately for the yellow-shirted Chelsea side, Wednesday midfielder Gary Megson had other ideas when he scored the winner from a free kick with just six minutes left.

More frustration was on the way the following Saturday when we played Middlesbrough at the Bridge. Boro had obviously come for a point and manager Malcolm Allison's defensive tactics, you'd have to grudgingly admit, paid dividends as the game ended in a tedious goalless draw. The Blues were profligate in front of goal in what was surely one of the worst matches seen at the Bridge that season. One incident of note was the injury to Clive Walker, who suffered a broken jaw when he was elbowed in the face by one of Boro's dead-eyed defenders. Little did we know that this would be Walker's last appearance for the Blues as Pat Nevin was waiting in the wings for his chance to claim a place in the regular starting line-up, which he grabbed with both hands. It was a sad turn of fate for Walker, who had the misfortune of being our star player during one of the bleakest periods in the club's history. A case, I suppose, of the right man at the wrong time.

After the final whistle blew against Boro, I decided to give my new girlfriend, Clare, a call to see what she'd planned for us that night. Of course, in those days there were no mobiles so I found the nearest phone box where, to my dismay, I was informed that a few of her girlfriends were coming down from London to spend the evening with us at her parents' home. She then said that we'd order a Chinese takeaway and all have a lovely evening. My heart sank. After the tedious 90 minutes that I'd endured that afternoon, the prospect of an evening with a bunch of females and just me, as the sole representative of the male species, was too much to bear. After ending the call, I was in a blind panic. What was I going to do? Then it came to me – a perfect get-out clause. I phoned my mate Tim, who'd been the lead guitarist in my previous band, and pleaded with him for help in carrying out my cunning plan, which went like this: Tim would phone Clare's home asking to speak to me, only to find that I was still on my way back from the football, whereupon Tim would ask Clare to get me to phone him back as soon as possible. Even though Tim was married, he was always up for a night out on the beer.

'You must save me,' I said. 'I need a drink.'

'Don't worry, mate. Your uncle Tim is coming to the rescue,' he assured me.

I was in no doubt that whatever Tim said would do the trick because he was, at that time, one of my closest mates.

He was also a cad and a pathological liar who, after just a couple of years of marriage, had already discovered that settling down definitely wasn't for him. Let's put it like this: Tim had a wandering eye, one that he was only too glad to follow at the slightest hint of female encouragement.

When I got to Clare's house, her mates had already turned up and I have to say that the noise was deafening, with each girl trying to get a word in above the hysterical girly laughter. I'd hardly got in the door when Clare said, 'You'd better phone your friend, Tim. He sounded really upset and wants you to call him back straightaway.'

'More trouble with Tracy, I should think,' I said with a look of concern on my face.

I then made the call to Tim, who it must be said gave a stellar performance. He went on to inform me that Tracy had left him, convinced that he was carrying on with someone.

'Just say "OK",' Tim whispered, which I duly did, trying to put as much worry into my voice as possible as he went on with his tales of woe.

I tried to bring our bullshit encounter to a close with a noble, 'Don't worry. Hold on. I'll be there.'

Tim's parting shot was, 'OK. Are you having your usual?'

'Of course,' I replied, the usual being a pint of Guinness with a whisky shot thrown in.

After putting the phone down, Clare asked me if everything was all right. I then proceeded to inform her of Tim's grim situation, that Tracy had walked out on him and that he needed to talk to someone.

'Oh, the poor thing,' Clare replied. 'You'd better go to him.'

'If that's OK with you?' I asked.

'Of course,' Clare said. 'I've got the girls here with me tonight.'

She'd barely finished that sentence before I was out of
the front door, on my toes, heading for a pint of Guinness
that had my name written all over it. Yes, I know it was
underhand, but the truth is, I bet, deep down, that Clare
was relieved as well as she was having an evening with all of
her mates without me to worry about. So, in a way, I firmly
believe in my heart, that in the end I did both of us a favour.

Clive Walker celebrates his second goal in Chelsea's epic victory over Liverpool in the FA Cup third round, January 1978 at Stamford Bridge.

Kenny Swain scores the first of his two goals against Spurs in the 2-2 draw at White Hart Lane, August 1978.

Bolton's Sam Allardyce puts through his own net to give Chelsea an amazing 4-3 win after trailing 3-0, October 1978.

Pop Robson scoring on his debut for the Blues in the 1-0 victory against Cambridge United at the Abbey Stadium, August 1982.

Clive Walker wheels away after scoring the vital goal against Bolton Wanderers at Burnden Park. This 1-0 win virtually saved Chelsea from relegation to Division Three, May 1983.

David Speedie celebrates scoring Chelsea's goal in the 1-1 draw against fellow promotion hopefuls, Newcastle, at St James' Park, March 1984.

Joey Jones, David Speedie and Kerry Dixon celebrate another goal in the 4-0 rout of Fulham at the Bridge, April 1984.

Kerry Dixon's brilliant effort against Leeds in the 5-0 victory in April 1984 – a result that confirmed Chelsea's promotion back to the top flight.

The management team of John Hollins, Ken Bates and manager John Neal celebrate Chelsea's return to the First Division, April 1984 – three of the men who were responsible for the upturn in the club's fortunes that season.

Photographic proof that Chelsea had a massive support back in those days as supporters crowd on to the pitch after gaining promotion against Leeds at the Bridge, April 1984.

Kerry Dixon celebrates scoring Chelsea's second goal in the 2-0 win over Manchester City at Maine Road, May 1984.

Kerry Dixon scores the Second Division title-winning goal against Grimsby at Blundell Park, 12 May 1984.

Chelsea players celebrate winning the Second Division title, May 1984, after five long years in the wilderness.

Chelsea's holy trinity of Speedie, Nevin and Dixon, seen here at the Café Royal where Pat Nevin received his Player of the Year award from chairman, Ken Bates, May 1984.

Yet more photographic evidence of Chelsea's tremendous away following as 20,000 Blues fans take over the Clock End at Highbury in the 1-1 draw against Arsenal, August 1984.

Kerry Dixon's iconic goal against Arsenal at Highbury, August 1984. This was Chelsea's first goal back in the top flight for five long years.

16

ON THE Tuesday after the Middlesbrough game, I flew out to Corfu for a week's holiday with our keyboard player, Dave, a holiday that was largely unremarkable except for one of the most bizarre episodes I've ever experienced. For the first few nights we were unaware that all of the nightlife was in a small town just along the coast called Benitses, which resulted in us wandering around the resort we were staying in with nothing to do apart from giving couples the evil eye as they stared lovingly at each other. Faced by this crushing boredom, we took the only way out that we could think of, and that was to get blind drunk. One night I decided to try James Bond's tipple, a vodka Martini, which certainly did the trick, and before too long I was already feeling the effects. Dave, on the other hand, went for the lethal combination of ouzo and cheap Metaxa brandy. I recall both of us being thrown out of a bar because Dave stole the owner's jaunty sailing cap. We were halfway down the road when the bar owner caught up with us and demanded his hat back. With a display of English arrogance, Dave threw the hat back at him, shouting, 'Have the bloody hat back, you stupid little git!' whereupon we headed back to our room.

Dave, who had more of a head for drink, carried on the night's excesses by taking a bottle of brandy to bed where he tried in vain to read his book, which usually resulted in him passing out with the book and his brandy glass crashing to the floor when, yet again, in the morning we'd have to clean up the broken shards. The last thing I remember of this particular night was again the sound of breaking glass on the tiled floor. After that I was out for the count. When I woke up with a predictable banging headache, I noticed a monogrammed white dressing gown, draped on the back of the chair. Where did that come from, I thought. I was certain it had nothing to do with me and it certainly wasn't the type of thing Dave would ever wear.

'Who does that belong to?' I enquired of Dave, when he eventually came round from the jolly-up.

'Oh, shit!' was his weak reply.

He buried his head back into his pillow. It was then that he proceeded to tell me what had happened after I'd fallen into my alcohol-infused sleep. Apparently he'd got up to sit on the balcony primarily to get some fresh air when he noticed said dressing gown on the back of a chair on the balcony of the room next door to ours. It was at that moment that he decided to borrow it, shall we say, and somehow climbed from our balcony to the adjoining one. What made his insane journey even more unbelievable was that our hotel was built on top of a cliff and it was a sheer drop down to the rocks below that surrounded the hotel's beach. How he managed that feat when he had drunk copious amounts of brandy and ouzo, God only knows.

Then the story became even more fantastical when he said that he'd spied through the wooden shutters the bloke in the room next door engrossed in sexual congress with some poor woman who Dave said was gasping for breath as the mountainous pile of flesh pumped away on top of her.

'Jesus!' I said.

'Yeah, he looked like a beached whale,' was Dave's reply.

I then enquired, 'Why?'

And he said, 'What do you mean – why?'

'Well, what the fuck did you nick that bloody dressing gown for?' I snapped back.

Dave looked bemused and wearily replied, 'To be honest, I have no idea.'

Now we had a problem. We couldn't return it to the balcony next door as it was broad daylight and anyway, the couple were sitting on their balcony having breakfast. Leaving it in the room wasn't a viable option because the maids came in every day to tidy up, and if anyone reported it missing, then we'd certainly be for the high jump. With very few options, we stuffed it into Dave's holdall along with all the other things that we'd be taking to the beach after breakfast.

When we arrived in the dining room, we were joined by a married couple from Bournemouth who we'd got friendly with.

'Have you heard?' said the wife.

'Heard what?' I enquired with a feeling of dread in my voice.

'Someone's stolen the owner's dressing gown, and apparently the maids are doing a room by room search, now.'

The bloody owner of all people, I thought, panicking.

'Who'd want to steal a dressing gown?' I asked.

'I don't know,' she went on to say. 'But apparently the owner's bloody furious.'

'Seeing that he paid a fortune for it!' chipped in the husband.

I looked at Dave, who I have to say looked sick. Somehow we were able to carry on with breakfast. During this, I noticed Dave moving the holdall further under the table. Seeing that we'd been in the next room to where the article of clothing went missing, you didn't need to be a brain surgeon to work out that as far as suspects go, me and Dave were certainly in the frame. How we managed to carry on a normal conversation with that married couple I'll never know. I'd certainly lost my appetite. I became convinced that the hotel staff were looking at us in a highly suspicious manner. When we left the breakfast table and were out of earshot, I asked Dave furiously, 'What the fuck are we going to do?'

'Don't worry,' he replied. 'I have a plan. Follow me.'

With very little choice, I tramped behind him to the beach. When we arrived I quickly enquired, 'Now, what's your bloody plan, then?'

'Right,' he said. 'Listen up. We hire a pedalo, take the holdall, and bury the dressing gown at sea, when we're far enough out. What do you think?'

'I think you're a fucking idiot for dropping us in the shit, if you want me to be brutally honest.'

'Well, what's your idea then?' he countered.

I had to admit that at that precise moment it did seem the only way out of our predicament, so grudgingly I acquiesced, and we made our way to hire a pedalo.

Finally we pedalled out to sea, all the time looking over our shoulders. When we were a considerable distance out, Dave said to me, 'That'll do. In you go.'

'You must be fucking joking,' I shouted. 'You got us into this shit. You can get us out of it.'

'Suit yourself,' was Dave's churlish reply. 'I'll go,' he said with a hint of exasperation, and promptly dived over the side and disappeared beneath the waves. When he resurfaced, he was holding a rock.

'Quick! Give it here!' Dave said. I quickly gave him the cursed dressing gown whereupon he tied it to the rock and disappeared back down into the depths. Finally, he resurfaced.

'It's done!' he exclaimed.

'Quick,' I said. 'Get on! There's a police pedalo pedalling towards us furiously! And I can see the blue light flashing.'

'Head for Albania,' Dave said. 'And don't spare the horses!' which we both found highly amusing as it seemed to break the tension we'd been under since first thing that morning.

And while it's funny to look back on that ludicrous episode, in hindsight things could have gone horribly wrong. Dave's moment of madness could have easily resulted in us being one of those headlines you hear about in the news of someone falling to their death while carrying out some daredevil stunt, under the influence of the sun and alcohol. Seriously, I'm pretty certain that if we'd been caught with that bloody dressing gown, the hotel owner, who went on to give us filthy looks for the rest of the week, would definitely have pressed charges against what he probably considered to be two arrogant Brits abroad displaying total disregard for other people's property.

The thought that me and Dave could have ended up in a Greek jail is not an outcome that the pair of us would exactly relish. Making a call home to my parents, telling them that I'd been banged up for stealing a dressing gown, would have been a huge embarrassment. Such was my paranoia for the rest of that holiday, I didn't feel totally safe until the plane took off from Corfu for the flight back to the dear old UK.

* * *

On the Saturday following my return, I made my way to Chelsea's next game – a London derby against Fulham at Craven Cottage. We'd won a League Cup tie 2-0 against First Division Leicester in midweek at Filbert Street. This result, coupled with a 3-2 win against Huddersfield, put the Blues in fine shape for the short trip to our local neighbours. I took up my place on the terrace right next to the actual cottage that gives the ground its name, and what a strange edifice this is to have stuck away in the corner of the ground. In fact, it resembles some of the cottage-like toilets you find in various London parks, which are used by certain dodgy individuals for their peculiar and nefarious habits, which made Fulham's nickname of the Cottagers highly dubious to say the least.

The whole of Craven Cottage was full of Chelsea, so much so that it almost seemed like a home game. I felt sorry in a way for the home side as their support was, in a word, pathetic. When Chelsea ran out they were wearing their all-yellow away strip, unlike the previous visit to the Cottage where we wore our normal all-blue kit. England manager Bobby Robson was there that day to take a closer look at Kerry Dixon, who'd been hitting the back of the net on a regular basis recently. Dixon didn't waste much time in his quest to impress Robson when he put Chelsea ahead after only nine minutes. Just the start we wanted. However, after 22 minutes, the Blues, or should I say yellows, found themselves 2-1 down after Gordon Davis hit a brace to put the home side ahead. And that's the way it stayed until, on the stroke of half-time, terrace favourite Joey Jones's header drew Chelsea level.

Four minutes into the second half, Pat Nevin was quickest to a blocked effort to score his first Chelsea goal to give the Blues the advantage. It looked all over when Colin Lee was put through and beat the Fulham goalkeeper with an angled drive to make it 4-2. Surely now we'd see it out. Unfortunately someone forgot to tell Fulham that the game was up, and Davis completed his hat-trick with 14 minutes left. Yet again time seemed to drag as the minutes ticked by at an agonisingly slow pace. I was convinced that

Fulham would equalise, but with just four minutes left Dixon grabbed the match-clinching goal. After his first effort was blocked, he somehow managed to wriggle his way back toward the goal to toe-poke the ball through a defender's legs into an empty net. The packed Chelsea end, in front of which he had scored, exploded into a frenzy, and a few minutes later the ref blew the whistle for full time with the final score of Fulham 3 Chelsea 5. What a great game it had been, and even to this day it still remains as one of my favourite away trips.

In Ken Bates's book, *Chelsea: My Year*, there's a photograph of the Chelsea end celebrating under the scoreboard, showing 5-3 to the Blues. I took a closer look at that photo and I could just about make myself out among the thousands of fans on that packed terrace. As the Chelsea players left the pitch that day, quite a few of them gave the clenched-fist salute that had so upset the media and Brighton when we'd made that same gesture to them back in August. I for one, and I'm sure that I speak for the majority of Chelsea supporters, saw it as a sign of unity, that we, as a club, and fans, were all in this together.

The following week I went to the Bridge to see us take on Cardiff City. In truth it was a largely forgettable game that we won 2-0 through Nevin's early strike, with Colin Lee then adding a second in the 63rd minute. As I recall, Cardiff offered little resistance and it was, as they say, a routine home win, a luxury that we hadn't enjoyed in goodness knows how many years. The one thing I can clearly remember was the appalling weather. For once, I gave up my place in front of the tea bar to stand in the Shed, which at least offered some protection from the driving rain.

During October 1983 we progressed in the League Cup, despite losing 2-0 at home to Leicester City, which meant that the overall aggregate score of the tie was now

2-2. I remember being absolutely gutted when Leicester scored their second goal just four minutes from full time, which then resulted in 30 minutes of extra time, and then the dreaded penalty shoot-out. Memorably, Welsh international Eddie Niedzwiecki came to our rescue, saving twice to earn a 4-3 shoot-out win. In all honesty, I really had little interest in our League Cup involvement, as the only thing that counted as far as all Chelsea fans were concerned was achieving promotion back to the First Division, which would mean a return to the top flight after five long years. Our only miss in that shoot-out was by David Speedie, who so far that season had had very little involvement, as he was unable to break up the striking duo of Dixon and Lee, who had been playing well together. It must have been really galling for Speedo considering he'd been one of our best players in the previous season's relegation battle. Now, of course, 1983/84 is remembered as being the season when the Dixon–Speedie partnership was formed and became one of the most deadly strike forces in Chelsea's history.

I was amazed when I checked and found out that it wasn't until 29 October 1983 that Dixon and Speedie actually started a league game together, when Charlton were the visitors to the Bridge. Speedo's impact was instantaneous as he gave us a 2-0 lead when he netted twice in the first half. The second half was uneventful, until Charlton pulled a goal back with 20 minutes left. Suddenly Chelsea looked nervous as Charlton, whose attacking threat had been practically non-existent, abruptly looked like they'd finally woken up and, sure enough, they equalised in the 75th minute. What had seemed to be a foregone conclusion was suddenly in grave doubt as Charlton surged forward in search of an unlikely winner. Perhaps it was their cavalier attitude that led to them being hit with a sucker punch when Dixon restored Chelsea's lead in the 78th minute and, despite some scares, the Blues saw out the remaining 12 minutes to take all three points. True, we'd made hard work of what seemed a nailed-on home win at half-time. But this Chelsea side were showing the tenacity and resolve to overcome any setback, gather themselves, and go on to win.

I left the Bridge that afternoon with a mood of celebration mixed with relief that somehow, despite blowing that two-goal lead, we'd eventually done enough to win what had turned out to be a hard-fought victory.

* * *

Our League Cup run came to an end when the Blues lost 1-0 to First Division West Bromwich Albion at the Bridge, Gary Thompson scoring the only goal of the game. The main concern for me when the final whistle blew wasn't the fact that we were out of the League Cup, but that the result might affect us in our next Second Division fixture, which was going to be one of our biggest games of the season when Newcastle United, one of the bookies' favourites for promotion, visited the Bridge. Newcastle had a team of seasoned pros that included the bubble-haired former England captain Kevin Keegan, and yet another of the curly permed brigade, Terry McDermott; the pair had been team-mates at Liverpool when they won the European Cup back in 1977. Their side also included future England internationals Chris Waddle and Peter Beardsley, who were beginning to make names for themselves.

There was a crowd of over 30,000 on what was a grey afternoon at the Bridge. This was feeling more like the old days when there was a sense of nervous anticipation around the ground. When the game kicked off, any worries we'd had that Chelsea might be overawed at the importance of the occasion were quashed when Nigel Spackman's drive put the Blues ahead in the eighth minute. Chelsea now smelled blood and proceeded to tear Newcastle to shreds, scoring a second when Peter Rhoades-Brown finished off a free-flowing move when he volleyed in at the far post. Any hopes that Newcastle may have had at half-time were extinguished when Speedie added Chelsea's third a minute after the restart. Keegan and co were looking completely shell-shocked as the home side gave them the runaround, and it came as no surprise when Speedie grabbed his second to put the Blues into an unassailable 4-0 lead. The most memorable moment, however, was Pat Nevin's mazy run when he seemed to take on the whole of the Newcastle team, not once, but twice. The only blemish on this dazzling display of dribbling was that it didn't result in a goal, but to all Blues fans it remains to this day one of the finest examples of that long-lost, and sadly missed, art. It brought back memories of the legendary Charlie Cooke in his pomp.

The Geordies were completely stunned at the final whistle as Keegan and his mates made their long, weary way down the tunnel. Apparently the story goes that Keegan had a word with Nevin about his attitude of trying to humiliate fellow professionals with that epic display of ball control, saying, 'You won't last long in this game if you try to take the piss like that,' which is a bit rich when you consider the actions of Keegan when he first burst on to the scene with Liverpool back in 1971 when he buzzed around the pitch like an angry wasp, giving seasoned pros the runaround with his all-action style. At this time, his opponents must have wondered who this little upstart was, who'd been signed from Fourth Division Scunthorpe. Today it seems unbelievable that someone from a lower-league side would go straight into the Liverpool first team and, within a year, win his first England cap. I can say without any fear of contradiction that it will never happen again in the modern game.

After that momentous victory over the Geordies, I decided to treat myself to a half a bottle of whisky as my hip flask of port and brandy, which by this time had become a ritual whenever I visited the Bridge, was running low. There were two reasons why I felt that I needed a drink that day, the first of which was one of celebration at the hiding we'd just dished out to Keegan and his mob. The second was more of a case of consternation at the thought that though Clare and myself had only been going out since May, cracks were already starting to appear in early November. I know they say that there is a honeymoon period when you can't see enough of each other, but in truth I can't remember ever feeling like that. It seemed that for both of us, it was just a relationship we both felt comfortable in; a sense of comfort that would continue to erode over the time that we were together. In fact, after Christmas, we split up for a few weeks to see how we felt. I know now that if you have to resort to that after just a few months together, then surely something is fundamentally wrong. Because both of us were scared of being thrown back into the world of being single we decided to give it another go, a decision that I regret to this day, and I have a sneaking suspicion that she is most probably of the same mind. And so the relationship staggered on for another couple of years until it ran its course. I can remember saying to one of my mates that my relationship with Clare had a date stamp on it, the only trouble being that I couldn't see the 'sell-by' date.

I can remember taking her to see Elvis Costello and the Attractions at the Hammersmith Odeon before Christmas 1983, in the hope that she might see the light, a tall order in retrospect, as she was a regular buyer of *Now, That's*

What I Call Music. She was also a fan of Phil Collins, that purveyor of coffee-table pap; surely one of the unlikeliest of pop stars ever to exist. At this time he was one of the most successful solo artists around, and there's no doubt that he had record sales that Elvis Costello could only dream about. But, as they say, there's no accounting for taste. I lost count of the evenings I'd spent in the company of Clare and her friends, interminable hours, listening to Collins warbling on about why his wife left him for a decorator. To add insult to injury I also had to endure the likes of Nik Kershaw, and the mind-numbingly boring Sade. I can remember one evening when I took off Collins's tawdry effort and put on Elvis Costello's *Imperial Bedroom*, which is a great album in my opinion. Grudgingly, they sat there and listened. I could see straightaway that they were uncomfortable with music that had some depth to it. No, this lot wanted music that was nothing more than a desperate sonic wallpaper. At the end of the track 'Town Crier', Clare's sister said, 'That's a nice song.'

I was just about to agree with her comment when someone said, 'That's enough of that. Let's put Phil on.'

At that moment, I could have wept. Unsurprisingly, Clare's visit to the Hammersmith Odeon never led to her becoming a Costello fan. Well, as they say, you can lead a horse to water but you can't make it drink.

By the time I got to Clare's house in Abbots Langley, I was decidedly the worse for wear. The mixture of a hip flask of port and brandy, topped up by a refill of Scotch, had certainly done its job. I felt comfortably numb, but thought rather foolishly that I mustn't let on that I'd been drinking, which in truth was stretching credibility a bit as I should imagine that I must have reeked like a distillery. When she opened the door, my cover was blown before I could even speak.

'Have you been drinking?' was her initial question. Before I could answer I disastrously tripped over the front doorstep and went flying past her into the hallway, executing a tremendous faceplant.

'You're drunk,' she said icily.

'How dare you cast aspersions about my good name,' I replied, which I found extremely funny and proceeded to break into hysterics. Unfortunately she didn't get the joke, and just stood there in the hallway until she marched purposefully into the front room. Needless to say the atmosphere for the rest of that evening was rather fraught.

The following Saturday Chelsea were at home to Crystal Palace, which on paper looked a far easier fixture than the Newcastle game. Logic seemed to say to me that we destroyed Newcastle, therefore mid-table nobodies like Palace should be no problem. Trouble is, football is a harsh mistress, and just when you think you've got it all sussed out it invariably comes back to kick you in the teeth. After just ten minutes one of the players we'd deemed as being surplus to requirements, full-back Gary Locke, who'd made such an impression on his Chelsea debut back in 1972, scored a goal that he could never have imagined, even in his wildest dreams. From 35 yards out, in front of the East Stand, he hit a dipping shot from far out on the right wing that tore past Eddie Niedzwiecki into the roof of the net. I don't think Eddie even saw it. Fifteen minutes later we found ourselves 2-0 down after an unfortunate defensive slip. There was a stunned silence around the Bridge broken only by the Palace fans celebrating. Then a total idiot standing next to me in front of the tea bar screamed out, 'You're shit, Chelsea. Fuck off!' which, seeing that we'd wiped the floor with fellow promotion hopefuls Newcastle seven days before, was an outburst that seemed extremely harsh, and was indicative of the Johnny-come-lately, that I'd never

ever seen before standing among the regulars in front of the tea bar.

It's strange, but when you stand in one place for so many years, you see all the old familiar faces each week, strangers who are bonded together by a common cause. I can recall in my first full season of going on my own to the Bridge, the cup-winning year of 1969/70, that there was a group of deaf blokes who used to stand just behind me. Every time there was a goal or a debatable decision, their sign language between all of them was a blur. What's really odd is that after that season I never saw them again, which is baffling as we'd just won the FA Cup – yet another question that will never be answered. I also stood next to a couple of kids that season who used to travel all the way up from Herne Bay, but yet again in 1970/71 they were nowhere to be seen. It was as though they'd just disappeared into the ether.

Somebody else standing near me that day against Palace really took exception to that ridiculous outburst by Bigmouth, and grabbed hold of him, spun him round, and bellowed into his face, 'Where were you last week, you fucking idiot? Not here. So keep your mouth shut!'

'I'm entitled to my opinion,' Bigmouth said weakly.

'Well, you can take your fucking opinion and stick it up your arse,' shouted his accuser, and with that, Bigmouth wisely departed the scene, never to return.

However, in the 37th minute, the veteran John Hollins pulled a goal back with a low drive into the Shed end goal. Now we were right back in it. The equaliser, when it came, was scored by David Speedie, who found the back of the net in the 63rd minute with a close-range effort. Despite absolutely battering Palace for the remaining 27 minutes, Chelsea couldn't find another goal but came close when Dixon hit the bar just before the final whistle. So while a draw was disappointing, apart from the usual crowd of morons like Bigmouth, after that savage rout of Newcastle none of us were really in a position to complain. Such are the vagaries of supporting a team. If you can't put up with the rough then it might be better for all concerned if you find some other sport to watch like carpet bowls, or shove-ha'penny.

17

OUR NEXT home game would be against another team in the promotion race, Manchester City, who were at the time a far different proposition than the current City side who nowadays seem to sweep all before them, except the Champions League of course, which has so far eluded them. I was going to mention Porto but decided against it as it might upset them. Personally, I thought that Chelsea and Sheffield Wednesday were the two main contenders for the title in 1983/84 with Newcastle and Manchester City left to fight it out for the last remaining place to ensure a return to the top tier of English football.

After gaining a 1-1 draw against dirty Leeds at Elland Road where Kerry Dixon netted what was in truth a bit of a gift of an equaliser, I spent the next week extolling Chelsea's virtues to my mate Mick about how well Chelsea were playing. Despite being a West Ham supporter, not the fanatical kind I should add, he said he'd be up for going to the City game with me, so on a sunny, early December afternoon we made our way to the Bridge. On the way there we stopped off at our usual watering hole, the King's Head and Eight Bells on Cheyne Walk, to indulge in a few drinks in a pub full of people who looked like they were fully paid-up members of the pink gin club. With not one Chelsea fan in sight it was a strange choice for a pre-match drink, a choice which I think had more to do with superstition, something that is endemic among football supporters; the pre-match ritual which must be adhered to at all costs. I remember we missed the kick-off, such was the interest in the game. There were massive queues trying to get into the ground. Finally we took up our position as ever in front of the tea bar. I noticed the BBC cameras were there, such was the growing interest in Chelsea's fortunes. Unfortunately the Blues decided to put on one of their most frustrating home performances of the season and fell behind just before half-time when Jim Tolmie's clever free kick caught Eddie Niedzwiecki by surprise and ended up in the back of the net at the Shed end.

The second half was one-way traffic as the Blues surged forward in search of an equaliser but no matter how hard they tried, that elusive goal would just not come. When the final whistle blew, City had come away with a priceless, if unexpected, victory. Typical, I thought. I'd been banging on to Mick all week about just how good Chelsea were, and now this. What a sickener.

Our plans for the evening were to go for a drink at The Cambridge on the corner of Shaftesbury Avenue, and then head to the nearest curry house to round off the night. I'm afraid I wasn't very good company as City had certainly put a dampener on that evening for me, and the curry, which in normal circumstances I would have really enjoyed, tasted like ashes in my mouth.

During that previous week, I'd given Mick the choice of going to the City game or coming with me to the next home match at the Bridge just three days later against Swansea. Unsurprisingly, he plumped for City, which was a more glamorous fixture. How I wished that those fixtures had been reversed as my fears that the home blip against City was the beginning of a poor run of form were dispelled when Chelsea murdered Swansea 6-1, with Paul Canoville – King Canners – netting a hat-trick. By half-time the Blues were already 3-0 up, and it seemed that poor old Swansea were being made to pay for Chelsea's disappointing display against City.

Going back to that City game, I can remember late in the second half Dixon broke clear down the right wing and was bearing down on the City goal at the Shed end, with Speedie racing into the box. A square pass seemed the logical choice for Kerry. Unfortunately he went for goal himself, which resulted in the unmarked Speedie – a man who had a notoriously short temper – seething with rage. It was actually years later that we found out that that incident against City led to the two of them coming to blows back in the dressing room. Thankfully they were pulled apart by team-mates, and found themselves hauled in later to be given a dressing down by manager John Neal, who firmly informed them that they'd have to find a way to work together as they were both integral to Chelsea's fortunes that season. Apparently the bad blood had been festering between the two of them all season, due to the fact that Speedo, who'd formed a strike partnership with Colin Lee in the previous campaign, was less than happy at being dropped for new boy Dixon to take his place.

On top of this, Speedo and Lee were good friends off the pitch which led to both of them, in some way, resenting Dixon's arrival at the Bridge. It clearly didn't help assuage that resentment when Kerry hit the ground running and couldn't stop scoring, which resulted in Speedo sitting on the bench from August to the end of October that year. Thankfully, the pair agreed to shake hands and put the team's best interests first, and went on to form one of the most fearsome strike partnerships in the club's history. In fact, in my opinion, their partnership was one that was only bettered by Ossie and Hutch, which was cruelly cut short by Hutch's terrible injury problems which led ultimately to his retirement at the age of just 27, a terrible blow for both the player and the club, and the thousands of Blues fans who idolised him.

The next home game would be in a fortnight on Saturday, 17 December 1983, a day that I will, like so many, never forget, because at 1.21pm the IRA detonated a car bomb outside Harrods, which resulted in six deaths and scores of injured bystanders. I was totally unaware of what had happened when I got to the Bridge. Back in those days before the internet and smartphones, news travelled more slowly. However, lots of people used to bring transistor radios to matches to keep up with the scores from elsewhere. I hadn't been standing there long before word spread of the explosion, which sadly came as no surprise as the cowardly IRA had been targeting London since 1973. It was another atrocity in a long list.

Apart from the terror of hearing this news, a horrible realisation engulfed me as I remembered that I'd told my mum and dad, and Clare, that I might visit Harrods to buy some of their luxury champagne toothpaste. Why? I have no idea, but had decided, unbeknownst to them, to give it a miss as I couldn't be bothered to divert from my trek to the Bridge. The only option open to me was to find a phone box as soon as the game had finished. It was quite chilling as there was a constant stream of announcements over the tannoy that certain people should go to the club offices immediately. No doubt a lot of people at the Bridge had friends and family who had gone to Harrods to do some Christmas shopping. I was distracted for the whole of the 90 minutes, and it seemed that Chelsea were suffering from the same malaise.

After taking a 2-0 lead through a Dixon penalty, followed by John Bumstead's fierce low drive in the 60th minute, the Blues looked home and dry. Then inexplicably, after Joe Waters pulled a goal back for Grimsby five minutes later, they proceeded to collapse alarmingly. Waters was by then a forgotten man of football. His only claim to fame was scoring two goals for Leicester City in their 2-0 FA Cup quarter-final win over QPR in 1974. Back then he was a fresh-faced youngster, but by 1983 he was definitely in the veteran stage of his career. Worse was to follow when ten minutes later, Grimsby scored two goals in two minutes to take a 3-2 lead. None of us in attendance could believe what we were witnessing. A game that had looked all but won now looked like a second home defeat in the space of a few weeks. Though Chelsea tried to rally and find an equaliser, it was not to be, and Grimsby came away with all three points. It had been a miserable afternoon all round but for once, instead of standing on the terraces waiting for the crowd to clear, I only had one thought on my mind, to get to a phone box as soon as possible to let everyone at home know that I was OK – a task that was easier said than done.

There were queues at every phone box I came across on my walk up Kings Road. It seemed that I wasn't the only one trying to let their families know that they were safe. Finally, when I got back to Victoria, I managed to find a phone box that was empty and called my mum and dad to let then know that their favourite son was still in one piece. Their relief was mixed with anger, especially when I told them that I'd decided against going to Harrods anyway.

'You stupid git!' my mum said, harshly. 'We've been out of our minds with worry. You'd better phone Clare. She's been phoning all afternoon. Just get out of London as soon as you can,' she demanded.

'Don't worry,' I replied. 'I'm on my way home now.'

I then phoned Clare who shall we say was not best pleased that thanks to my actions, I'd sent her and my parents into a blind panic.

Victoria was packed with tourists that evening, carrying their suitcases, all desperately trying to get out of the capital. British Rail must have made a mint that night as all of the trains were jam-packed, such was the fear that the IRA inflicted on innocent people back in those days. I didn't really feel safe until my train from Euston started on its way back to Hertfordshire. The fact that Chelsea had lost would normally have left me in a foul mood. But for once, events had alleviated my despair at the result, and I was just glad that I'd made it out of London safely. To have become a victim of the IRA, because I'd wanted to buy champagne toothpaste, to all intents and purposes, would have been too bizarre to contemplate.

* * *

The Blues got back on track the following week with a fine 4-2 win against Shrewsbury at Gay Meadow, with two late free kicks from John Bumstead sealing the points. Our Christmas fixtures that year were a strange mixed run of results. Less than 24 hours after our win at Shrewsbury, we were at home to Portsmouth for an 11.30am kick-off. I remember this day as being the start of our trouble with penalties that blighted us for the next few years. The game itself was a see-saw affair with the Blues trailing twice, only to level things up by half-time. Sandwiched in between this flurry of goals was a penalty miss by Kerry Dixon, which was saved by the Pompey keeper.

Kerry got the chance for redemption on the hour when the Blues were awarded another spot kick. The Bridge was hushed as he stepped up to take his second penalty of the day but to our horror, Kerry's effort hit the crossbar.

There was a silence around the stadium apart from the Portsmouth mob, celebrating their second escape from jail in one afternoon. And 2-2 was the way it stayed. True, we hadn't lost, but with two penalties missed it almost seemed like a defeat.

On New Year's Eve we were at home again. This time the visitors were Brighton, who proceeded to defend in depth to nullify the strike force of Dixon, Speedie and Nevin. Their negative tactics seemed to be paying off until the 50th minute when the Blues were awarded yet another penalty. Surely Kerry wouldn't take this one but no, there he was, taking responsibility once again as he placed the ball on the spot. The thought of those two penalty misses surely must have still been on his mind. I thought, it took some guts to step up once more but sadly for Kerry, the curse struck again as he missed his third spot kick in successive games, his effort being saved by veteran keeper Joe Corrigan. The Bridge was once again stunned into silence. Poor Kerry just stood there, a forlorn and lonely figure.

It looked like another two points would be dropped for the second successive home game. That was until the 77th minute, when Speedie fired the Blues ahead with a close-range effort at the Shed end. There were joyous scenes all around the Bridge, apart from the Brighton supporters, who had come to the match that day on their tandem. Then to round the afternoon off nicely, that shrinking violet Jimmy Case, the ex-Liverpool player, was sent off for Brighton in the closing minutes. It had been a close-run thing but when the final whistle blew, Chelsea had gained a priceless 1-0 victory.

Two away defeats followed. The first was against Middlesbrough at Ayresome Park, where the Blues lost 2-1 after Eddie Niedzwiecki's mistake in the last few minutes.

A week later we were dumped out of the FA Cup in the third round, by Blackburn Rovers at Ewood Park with the home side scoring the only goal of the game, although apparently Chelsea had a perfectly good goal chalked off after Dixon was adjudged to have fouled their keeper in the process of netting. So while it was a disappointment to go out of the cup at the first hurdle, at least it left us, as the time-honoured saying goes, with just the league to concentrate on.

John Neal's reaction to these back-to-back losses on the road was one of the most astute moves by any Chelsea manager when he signed Stoke City's Micky Thomas for £75,000. Thomas was an all-action, bustling midfielder, blessed with a brilliant engine to get up and down the pitch from minute one to the final whistle. He was just the type of player we needed to make that promotion push in the remaining months of the season. I have to say that Thomas was one of those players, like his team-mate Joey Jones, who you loathed when he was playing for the opposition but loved once he'd pulled on your shirt. On Saturday, 21 January 1984, Thomas made his Blues debut against Derby County at the Baseball Ground. In a hard-fought match that was played on a mud-heap of a pitch and in a second-half blizzard, Chelsea came away with all three points after a fine 2-1 win to put us back on track after our recent setbacks.

Just seven days later, Sheffield Wednesday arrived at the Bridge for what looked like a showdown for the Second Division title. Chelsea tore into the brutish Wednesday side right from the kick-off, and in the 16th minute Thomas scored the first of his two goals that afternoon to become an instant cult hero. There were ten minutes left when Pat Nevin put Chelsea into what looked like an unassailable 3-0 lead, but Wednesday had other ideas and scored two goals in three minutes to ensure a nail-biting finish. The relief when the referee blew the final whistle was overwhelming as Chelsea took all three points after a pulsating 3-2 win. In truth, though I'm biased, Chelsea looked a class above Wednesday whose main game plan was to batter the ball forward at every opportunity, with very little build-up. To me, and many others, their tactics were a bit of a stain on the beautiful game. Alongside the likes of Watford and Wimbledon, their play would soon come to be known as route-one football, something that I'm glad to say Chelsea never resorted to. The 35,147 crowd was the best of the season, and once more there was the feeling that this could be our year to escape the prison that had been the Second Division for the last five years.

To celebrate, I bought the classic blue home shirt after this game, to go with the yellow away shirt I'd bought earlier in the season. For some strange reason I wore the yellow shirt more than the blue one, and it remains one of my favourite Chelsea shirts of all time.

That victory over Wednesday meant that Chelsea sat proudly at the top of the table. The following Saturday we had a chance to claim our second scalp from Yorkshire when Huddersfield were the visitors to the Bridge, and once again the Dixon and Speedie partnership earned the points with Kerry grabbing a brace and David netting the third in a comfortable 3-1 win, a result that meant the Blues retained their place as league leaders.

* * *

Apart from the game, the most notable memory I have of that day is bumping into one of my old school-mates, Eddie. We started banging on about our school days in the 1960s and remembered two standout incidents which must have occurred when I was about 11 years old in

1966. Like a lot of boys in those days, we were obsessed by World War Two. Anything and everything concerned with that conflict interested us. While it was the German uniforms and weapons that fired our imaginations, there was one British regiment that stood out for us at the time – the Parachute Regiment, the Red Devils. They had a different uniform to the regular army, and the helmet looked bloody brilliant. For instance, one of my mates' dads had fought at the legendary Battle of Arnhem in 1944, and still had his paratrooper helmet. One by one, we would go round to see my mate and try the helmet on. Five minutes was the allotted time that we were allowed to wear it for, in case his parents, especially his dad, came home. So besotted were we by the tales of derring-do of the Parachute Regiment that we used to practise jumping off garage roofs, and, much to my nan's anger, the wall outside her house, replicating the roll you had to do to land safely.

At that time in the 1960s, war films were the big draw at the cinema, and I saw the lot; *The Guns of Navarone*, *The Great Escape*, *633 Squadron* and *Operation Crossbow*, not forgetting the schoolboys' number one favourite, *Zulu*, which blokes of my age still hold in great reverence. So consequently, following our so-called parachute training, me and Eddie decided to go to the local army cadet barracks to sign up. To be honest, I think both of us were scared that we might be accepted. As far as I was concerned I was much too young to be leaving all of my home comforts behind to go jumping out of aeroplanes. The trouble was that neither of us wanted to be the one to say, 'Let's just go home.' We found ourselves at the barracks, informing one of the young soldiers that we needed to speak to the CO. After a brief wait, we were marched into his office.

'What can I do for you, lads?' the officer said.

'We want to join up,' was our nervous reply.

'How old are you, boys?'

'Eleven,' we replied in unison.

'Well,' he said. 'You're a bit too young to be enlisting. Why don't you come back in a few years? We'd be glad to have you when you're both old enough.'

'Sorry,' Eddie said. 'We won't be coming back here. We want to join the Parachute Regiment.'

'A noble ambition,' remarked the CO. 'But it would be better if you joined the army cadets first. The Parachute Regiment is an elite unit.'

'Can't we just join the Parachute Regiment?' I pleaded.

The CO was by this time growing impatient, and said, 'OK, boys. Go home and talk it over with your parents and see what they say.'

We were then promptly dismissed.

Strangely, me and Eddie never went back. Just as well, on my part, as I later discovered I was terrified of heights. When I was in my 20s I was asked by one of my mates if I fancied doing a sponsored parachute jump. My first reaction was a feeling of nausea, swiftly followed by a reply in the negative. Eddie, however, did pursue a career in the military and was actually in the navy for a few years.

At the beginning of 1967 Eddie and myself were up to mischief yet again. As well as war films, there was also a craze for the spy genre. Ever since the first Bond film, spy adventures had caught the imagination of small boys across the land. Having seen films like *Dr No*, we then all went to see *Goldfinger*, and *From Russia With Love*. There were also cash-in films such as the *In Like Flint* movies with James Coburn. There was also *The Ipcress File* with the Harry Palmer character played by Michael Caine, which I must admit went over a young boy's head – too much talking, I thought, and not enough gunfire. But there was no doubt that the American TV series *The Man From U.N.C.L.E.* was *the* spy adventure that captured our hearts, with Robert Vaughn playing the brilliantly named Napoleon Solo, and English actor David McCallum playing, of all things, a Russian agent called Illya Kuryakin. As soon as the programme hit the TV screens in the UK, boys of my age were hooked. Like many others, I bought the show's shoulder holster, and even wore it under my blazer in assembly one morning as our notoriously pious headmaster tried to indoctrinate us in more of his cock-eyed religious beliefs.

All of this led to me and Eddie hatching another plot to make some more mischief. One of our class-mates, Phil, was, how shall I put it, gullible. So we decided that he would be the perfect victim for our jolly jape. Somehow we convinced him that Eddie and myself were members of a secret spy order called The Assassins. We went on to tell him lurid tales of the missions that we'd carried out, and the clandestine meetings that were held once a week. You might think that Phil was an idiot to believe such a load of old bullshit, but boys of that age will believe anything if it's their deepest desire, and as it turned out, Phil was indeed champing at the bit to join The Assassins.

When he asked what he had to do to become a member of our select group, we told him that first of all there was an initiation ceremony where he would be blindfolded, led into a secret chamber where he had to stand alone, with a wet towel draped over his head, while the other members of The Assassins would smack him round the face, one by one.

'I don't like the sound of that,' complained Phil.

'Well, me and Eddie have gone through it,' I said. 'So, if you're not interested, well let's just forget about it.'

'No! no,' said Phil. 'When's the next meeting?'

'It's next Wednesday,' I blurted out.

'Whereabouts?' asked Phil. For some reason, my mind went blank. All I could think of was to say, 'It's at the community centre. Be there at 7.30.'

'Will you be there?'

'Of course,' I said. 'But we can't talk to you about the initiation taking place. Our identities, like yours, will have to be kept hidden at all costs.'

'What do I get when I'm in?' asked Phil. Quickly, I had to think.

'You get a golden glove,' I unbelievably replied.

'Where are yours, then?' questioned Phil. Before I could come up with an answer, Eddie chipped in, 'We're only allowed to wear them at meetings, or when we're on a mission.'

Not long after this, the bell went to announce that the school day had finished, and such are the vagaries of young boys that by the time I'd got home I'd forgotten about our ludicrously tall tale, and over the next few days it was never mentioned.

On the following Wednesday I went to the pictures with my mum and my sister Elaine. During that period in the 1960s we were regular cinema-goers, and it's hard to imagine now but I saw all of the big films of that decade. That lovely aroma when you walked into the foyer, of hotdogs and popcorn, and a Kia-Ora orange drink, made a visit to the cinema a memory I still cherish to this day.

I can't recall what we saw that night. Perhaps it was another war film. Then again, it might have been one of those family films that I dreaded going to see. Maybe it could have been one of those awful 1960s swinging London cash-ins, like *Smashing Time*, with Rita Tushingham and Lynn Redgrave, which portrayed a London that frankly, I'd never seen during my time living in the capital.

When we got on the bus home we sat on the lower level of the double-decker, which my mum preferred to the upper deck. In those days it would be full of committed smokers, puffing away. As we approached the main bus stop, I saw to my horror Phil, standing in the bus shelter. Bloody hell, I thought, he believed us. Quick as a shot, I jumped out of my seat, and said to my mum and sister, 'One of my mates is just getting on. I'll just go and say hello.' I swear I'd never run as fast as I did down the aisle of the bus that night. I managed to stop Phil as he stepped up on to the bus, and said, 'Let's go upstairs.' The sweat was pouring off me as I explained to him that the meeting of The Assassins had been called off at the last minute as there had been a security breach.

I'd already been in trouble earlier that year by aiming my uncle's deactivated Lee Enfield rifle at the neighbours' kids. It seemed that during those days, trouble and myself went hand in hand. What made it worse was that Elaine was a model child. I was the polar opposite to this. I was always causing worry for my mum and dad. I was, to put it bluntly, a pain in the arse. I can remember my dad saying to me with an air of desperation, 'Why can't you just blend in? Why has it always got to be you?'

Sadly, I never managed to just blend in. Even to this day, the saying 'show me the boy at five, and I'll show you the man' is in my case highly applicable.

Thankfully, there were no repercussions regarding Phil joining The Assassins, and me and Eddie decided it would be best all round to completely drop the subject.

18

BY THE time Chelsea travelled to Newcastle on Saturday, 10 March 1984, they still sat proudly at the top of the table. The Geordies were giving it large for the game and had sworn revenge for the 4-0 mauling they'd received at the Bridge earlier in the season. But despite all of that big talk, Chelsea, playing in their all-yellow away strip, came away from St James' Park with a creditable 1-1 draw with David Speedie having fired them ahead. It took an unlucky slip by Micky Thomas to let in Terry McDermott to level for Newcastle. Both teams had chances to win the game, with Chris Waddle spurning a glorious chance for the hosts in the dying minutes, but he blazed his effort way over the bar, perhaps getting in some practice for his horrendous penalty miss for England in the World Cup semi-final against West Germany in 1990.

Chelsea remained in pole position the following Friday when on a bitterly cold evening, we beat Blackburn Rovers 2-1 at the Bridge, gaining some revenge for our FA Cup third-round exit to the same opponents. Chelsea's second goal that night was perhaps the best of the season so far when Speedie's dipping, long-range effort found the back of the net to give us a 2-0 half-time lead. And though Blackburn pulled a goal back with 20 minutes left, the Blues saw out the game comfortably. It was now becoming apparent that, barring a total collapse on the run-in, Chelsea were in a good position not only to get promotion, but to win the title as well, something we just missed out on back in 1976/77 when we'd finished runners-up to Wolves. Though promotion was the priority, it would be nice this time if we could actually get our hands on a trophy as it had been 13 long years since a major prize had come to the Bridge.

The fear that we might make a mess of the run-in came the following Saturday when Chelsea found themselves 3-0 down to Cardiff after just 25 minutes. And that's the way the score remained at Ninian Park with just six minutes left. I was keeping up with the scores that day on my radio. I actually turned it off with ten minutes to go, finally accepting that it was just going to be one of those days. In a desultory mood, I went downstairs to the front room where my dad was watching *Grandstand*, waiting for the results to come in on the vidiprinter.

'How are they getting on?' my dad asked.

'Bloody well losing 3-0, for fuck's sake.'

'Well,' my dad said, 'you can't expect them to win every week.'

'Why not?' was my curt reply.

When Chelsea's score came through, I couldn't believe my eyes as I read Cardiff 3 Chelsea 3. Surely this was a mistake. It must be a mistake. I waited until the full-time classifieds were announced at five o'clock before I would believe that that incredible scoreline was, indeed, correct. I later found out that Kerry Dixon had started the comeback in the 84th minute. That was followed a minute later when Colin Lee, who had by now been converted to a full-back, grabbed Chelsea's second. I've seen footage of that game on YouTube, and for the last few minutes it was nothing short of a tidal wave of yellow shirts as Chelsea pressed for the equaliser. Cardiff looked shell-shocked as a game they'd thought was already won was in danger of slipping away from them. Their fears were confirmed when Chelsea were awarded a penalty in the 90th minute. This time Nigel Spackman took responsibility and joyously thumped the ball home from the spot. A result like this the previous season would have been unthinkable, as we'd most probably have thrown the towel in, but yet again this team had proved that it had a steely resolve to overcome adversity in their desire to get the club back to where it belonged.

A lot of credit should go to manager John Neal and his assistant Ian McNeill for the inspired recruitment during the summer of 1983. One should also mention good old Ken Bates, the abrasive chairman, for funding these acquisitions. Like all successful teams, Chelsea had a strong spine starting with goalkeeper Eddie Niedzwiecki, a leader in Joey Jones in defence, two solid centre-backs in Pates and McLaughlin, a tireless midfield with the likes of Nigel Spackman, John Bumstead and the inspired signing of Micky Thomas, who had fitted into the midfield seamlessly for the second half of the season, then up front you had two deadly strikers in Dixon and Speedie. Perhaps the icing on the cake was wee Pat Nevin, the mercurial 19-year-old Scottish winger who had been nothing short of a revelation. I'd put Nevin in the same bracket as Charlie Cooke and Eden Hazard as some of the finest exponents I've ever seen of that lost art of the game, dribbling with the ball.

Nowadays, all you seem to see for the most part is the philosophy of pass and move, which often reminds me of all the thrills that you can get in watching a game of chess, a game where you have no idea of what the rules are. It's true to say that I find some of the matches I watch today tedious to say the least. Of course, there is the odd exception like the 2-2 draw with Spurs in the 2015/16 season, when we ended any hopes of that loathsome mob from north London winning the Premier League. That result, when we came back from 2-0 down to give Leicester the title, is a vivid memory. That beautiful sight of Hazard's shot eight minutes from time, flying past the sulky Spurs keeper Hugo Lloris, is one that I will always treasure. This match has gone down in football history as the 'Battle of the Bridge' because, basically, the hatred that exists between the two clubs became glaringly obvious as both sides proceeded to kick lumps out of each other. I have to say that Spurs were the main culprits, when they completely lost their heads as their chance of the title went up in smoke. Unsurprisingly, I enjoyed every minute of that game. At least there was some passion. Both teams played with fire in their bellies, something that you see less and less of in modern football, which is often bland and, in a word, beige.

* * *

On Saturday, 7 April 1984, Chelsea were at home to Fulham. I went to the game with my mate Dave, our keyboard player. Dave was a Manchester United supporter who happened to have been born in Yorkshire. I asked him if he'd ever heard of the War of the Roses, but my enquiry was met with silence. He'd also gone to school in Fulham and proffered that he had a soft spot for them. Unfortunately for him, the only soft spot that day was the Fulham defence as Chelsea's quicksilver football ripped them to pieces. Kerry opened the scoring in the first minute, and from then on it was nothing less than a rout. By half-time Chelsea led 3-0, with Speedo grabbing a goal that was sandwiched in between a brace scored by Kerry.

During the week, the Fulham boss Malcolm Macdonald had said in the papers that he didn't rate the

Blues, and fancied his Fulham side to come away with something from the Bridge. Big-mouth Macdonald was known for opening his trap and putting his foot in it. In the three major cup finals he'd played in for Newcastle and Arsenal, he announced to everyone who could be bothered to listen what he was going to do to his opponents. Sadly for Supermac the only thing he managed to do in all three finals was to pick up three runners-up medals after giving performances that bore a striking resemblance to the Invisible Man. I'm not saying that he wasn't an effective centre-forward – he was, with his physical strength and bursts of speed, but the fact that the highlight of his career was scoring all five goals for England in their victory over those giants of football, Cyprus, tells you all you need to know about yet another flat-track bully. The second half was still dominated by Chelsea, and they managed to add to their tally when Nevin's deflected shot beat Fulham keeper Gerry Payton.

My other vivid memory of that afternoon was that when Speedo smashed in the second goal, there was a bloke standing near us who looked suspiciously like he'd had a skinful. He was stuffing a burger into his mouth. Whenever Chelsea looked like they were on the attack, lumps of burger were falling out of his mouth as he roared the Blues on. When Speedo's shot hit the back of the net he couldn't contain himself any longer, resulting in an explosion of bun and burger meat hitting everyone standing in his vicinity. I noticed on my jacket that there were globules of tomato sauce and mustard, with half-chewed bits of bread. It was totally disgusting. Behaviour that would have been considered appalling outside a football ground was instantly forgiven by all the Chelsea supporters standing around him as, to a man, we were all joined together in the love of our team. There were no more goals that afternoon, and

Fulham – and their boastful manager – left the scene of their humiliation with their tails firmly between their legs, to reflect on the 4-0 drubbing that the Blues had inflicted upon them.

That evening, we went for a drink in Covent Garden at the Punch and Judy. All went well until, upon leaving the pub, I inadvertently opened my jacket which revealed my blue Chelsea home shirt. Within an instant, half a dozen beered-up Geordies started chasing us, shouting dire threats of what they were going to do to these two Cockney bastards. Thankfully we managed to outrun them and for all I know, they're still looking for us to this day. It seemed that Newcastle's 3-1 victory against Charlton that day had done nothing to dispel their hatred for Chelsea, who'd absolutely battered them during one of their earlier visits to the capital, obviously a wound that cut very deep and showed no signs of healing.

* * *

Around this time with work in the building trade drying up, I found myself in need of a job, as the retainer I was receiving from the music publisher was only sufficient to allow you a diet of bread and water. I was leaving my home one day for a look round the different building firms to ask if they had anything going for painters and decorators and was walking down my garden path when I heard the phone ringing. Quickly, I let myself back in to find that it was one of my old college mates, Chris, on the phone asking if I'd be interested in a contract that would last until July. It was at a new firm called Microdata, on the Hemel Hempstead industrial estate. The work would be painting and decorating, and a bit of maintenance. It was a huge complex that was still empty, the plan being that we'd get it into shape before all the computer geeks and pointy-heads moved in. Needless to say I bit his hand off, especially since Chris informed me that a couple of the other lads I went to building college with would be joining us. Another couple of minutes and I would have missed that chance to experience one of the best, yet weirdest, jobs I ever had.

On that first morning, I met up with the other lads from college and some other blokes who I'd never seen before. My God, what a motley crew we were. On the first day, two of them were given their marching orders for stealing some of the maintenance geezers' tools. Then there was another bloke who we christened 'Harry the Hatchet', who was sporting a heavy bandage on his right arm.

'How did you do that?' we asked.

'Well,' he said, 'the wife kicked me out last night, saying that I'd been playing around. To be fair, she'd got a point because I'd been a naughty boy – again.'

After being thrown out, he'd gone to the pub, got bevvied up and then decided to go home and batter the locked and bolted front door down with an axe he kept in his van. Unfortunately for him, due to the alcohol he'd consumed, he missed the door with the axe and put it straight through a glass panel, causing it to explode into tiny, yet deadly shards of glass that cut his arm to ribbons. He'd spent the night in A&E but still managed to turn up for work that morning.

Auf Wiedersehen, Pet had been the big TV hit in the UK the previous year, and now it seemed that I was in the real-life version of it. The job itself was a complete doss. After doing some work, you could lose yourself in the myriad of empty rooms in that huge edifice. One of my college mates, Melvin, used to disappear every morning at about 11 o'clock, and wouldn't be seen until after lunch. We named him 'Shalamar Melv' after the band Shalamar, who had a song in the charts at the time called 'Disappearing

Act', which seemed very apt for Melvin due to his daily disappearances into thin air.

While working on the contract, it became obvious that there was no love lost between the Microdata maintenance staff and us contractors, who they thought were a bunch of chancers. We thought, when it came to skiving, we were rank amateurs to the lazy sods in their maintenance department, who did virtually nothing all day except have countless brews, and then disappear for hours in their vans to God knows where. Two of them in particular loathed us, and when I say 'us', it seems that me, Chris and Melvin were the main protagonists who caused their venom and bile. Yet I have to admit that we were smartarses, who always seemed to have an answer. One of the maintenance men, Stan, despised our little trio with a pathological passion.

'You're just a bunch of fucking clowns, you three,' was one of his daily insults.

'You're just jealous of our good looks,' Chris would reply.

'There's no way I'm jealous of you fucking knobheads,' shouted Stan.

'Well, you should be,' Melvin snapped back, 'because you've got a face that looks like an arsehole turned inside out.'

Looking back, it's a wonder that those daily flare-ups didn't turn into physical violence.

We finally managed to get our own back on Stan after we'd found out that he'd been visiting management on a constant basis to get the three of us sacked. We'd noticed that Stan would always go for his morning dump after the tea break, with newspaper under his arm, supposedly to read while he took care of business. We'd been working in those toilets, giving them a fresh coat of paint, when we became aware that if you turned the lights out you literally couldn't see your hand in front of your face. With no windows in those loos it was, as they say, pitch black. So one day, as Stan made his way to the toilets for his daily doings, we followed him and waited until he'd settled himself on the toilet seat preparing to unload what was on his mind. Silently we crept up to the door, and as quick as a flash turned the light off. We just had time to hear Stan screaming 'no', before he was enveloped in his very own Black Hole of Calcutta.

God knows how he managed to finish the job, but when he came back he was apoplectic. His accusations were aimed at us but we flatly denied having anything to do with that sorry episode. Stan, however, had no doubts as to who the culprits were, and for the rest of our time working there the relationship between him and us was, to put it mildly, tense.

The other bloke who had a problem with the contractors was Ron, who didn't stop for one minute in showing his contempt for us. I had no idea why, as the staff of Microdata were earning more than the contractors anyway. Ron was in truth an overweight blowhard, who couldn't and wouldn't stop bragging about what he was earning each week. He even stooped so low as to count out his wage packet in front of us, just to let us know what a bunch of idiots we were, to work for less. He was the embodiment of the great British workman, who spent his working life being busy doing nothing.

There was also the fact that there was a big drug culture on that job, especially among the contractors. It didn't help that speed was the drug of choice which didn't benefit our mental health one iota. Every Friday we collected our supply of whizz for the week from one of the electricians who used to dish out our requirements in matchboxes. Personally, I was a bit of a lightweight, and I only used to drop one or two tabs at a time, while some of my mates were speeding off their nut every day. If all this seems a bit wild, then try to imagine what it was like in the UK then. For instance, we had Margaret Thatcher and her cronies inflicting their draconian rules on the working man, especially the miners in closing down their pits, and essentially ruining communities overnight. These were the days when you saw police on the six o'clock news baton-charging these miners and beating the life out of them. It was a time of high unemployment, so a job like that contract, for however long it would last, was a godsend. Of course, we knew it wouldn't last forever, and in July of that year all the contractors were told that their services were no longer required. I doubt if jobs like that exist anymore. It's hard to believe that we actually got paid double time for working on a Saturday, and treble time for working on a Sunday, and, what's more, there was hardly anything to do when working at the weekends. We spent a lot of the time playing pool, meaning I can say with confidence that I've actually been paid money for playing that game, for hours on end.

After the job finished, it was back to looking for another contract. In Melvin's case I only ever saw him once more, when he went past in a really nice Mercedes, so he'd obviously fallen on his feet. As for Chris, the only time I ever saw him again was on a trip up to Euston where I was travelling to the Bridge to watch a 3-3 draw with Liverpool in the spring of 1987. This was a game that turned out to be the last time Speedo scored for the Blues, and what a goal it was: a dipping half-volley.

Going back to 1984, one abiding memory I have of that year is the craze that summer of people wearing black-and-white-checked shirts, which seemed to be everywhere. Why? Who knows. Just one of those fleeting fashion crazes that was here one moment and gone the next. It was also the

year of the 'Frankie Says Relax' T-shirts which seemed to
be everywhere. This was after the track 'Relax' by Frankie
Goes to Hollywood had been a massive hit. Personally, I
detested that song, and as far as I was concerned, Frankie
could say what he liked. I, for one, wasn't bloody listening.

19

CHELSEA'S NEXT game in the run-in was against Shrewsbury at the Bridge on Easter Saturday, 21 April 1984. I'd already committed to going to Lulworth Cove with Clare earlier in the year, so it was all booked and paid for. There was no way that I could wriggle out of this trip. Lulworth Cove is a beautiful place but, unsurprisingly, my mind was still on Chelsea, and how they were getting on that afternoon. It was a gloriously sunny spring day.

Clare said, 'Let's go and have a cream tea.'

'Good idea,' I replied.

When we got into the tea room it was all very genteel, something that resembled that scene in *Withnail and I* when Richard E. Grant and Paul McGann, playing two out-of-work actors, drunkenly asked for cake 'and the finest wines known to humanity', much to the horror of the sedate customers sitting nearby. At about 3.15pm I was on the receiving end of withering looks, both from Clare and the rest of the customers, when I put on my Walkman plus headphones to see how Chelsea were doing.

'You've got to be joking,' Clare said with a hint of exasperation in her voice.

'Sorry,' I said, 'but I have to see how the boys in blue are getting on.'

Clare sat there in a sulk but that didn't stop me one bit. I then found out that Kerry had given us the lead in the sixth minute.

'We're one up,' I told her, a comment that was met by a deafening silence on her part. Realising that it was a bit unfair to ruin her cream tea, I removed the Walkman until half-time. By the time we'd finished the tea and scones and sat outside in the sunshine, once more the Walkman was back on my head and I found out that Chelsea were now leading 2-0 at the break, Pat Nevin scoring the second.

Once again I was forced to remove my headphones, and I sat through the second half completely disinterested in what was going on around me. On more than one occasion I was so far away that it almost felt that I was standing in my usual place in front of the tea bar, watching the Blues taking another mighty step to the Second Division title. Though Clare was chatting away, I hardly heard what she was prattling on about. Her mouth was moving, but so worried was I about the game that she might as well have been talking to a brick wall. At 4.50pm I put the Walkman on to find out that the Blues had won comfortably, 3-0, with Kerry scoring his second goal three minutes from time. The only negative was that, yet again, we'd missed our customary penalty when Nigel Spackman's shot was saved by Steve Ogrizovic, the Shrewsbury keeper. Well pleased with the result, I could at long last enjoy the sunshine and bathe in the warm glow of Chelsea's victory.

That result meant that a win at Fratton Park against Portsmouth on the following Tuesday would see us promoted. I knew it would be a tough game, as Portsmouth had been a bit of a handful at the Bridge when they'd come away with a hard-fought 2-2 draw. Mind you, we gave them a helping hand that day because of Kerry's two missed penalties. Unable to go to the game because of work, I'd planned to meet up with my old band-mates in a pub in Harpenden. Of course, in those days, there was very little live football on TV, so I had to keep nipping out to the car to listen to the radio to see how the Blues were getting on. It was packed in the pub but that didn't stop me from pushing my way through the crowd to get the latest updates.

At half-time, Chelsea were leading 1-0 through Micky Thomas's fifth-minute header, which meant that as it stood they were now just 45 minutes away from being promoted. About ten minutes into the second half I was back in the car just in time to hear that Chelsea had been awarded a penalty after Nevin's overhead kick had been handled on the line. Nervously, I waited. Would this be yet another disaster from the penalty spot? To my unbridled joy, wee Pat converted and the yellow-shirted Chelsea players were now on the brink of what we'd dreamed about all season. I then decided I'd give it another 15 minutes and check in again.

I told my mates my joyous news but seeing that none of them supported Chelsea, my glad tidings were met with overwhelming indifference. Unable to bear the tension, I decided that my next visit to find out the score would be my last, as my mates seemed perfectly capable of enjoying themselves without a nervous wreck like myself ruining their evening. When I returned to the car and turned on the radio, I got the shock of my life to find out that Pompey had pulled back the two-goal deficit and were now level. There was a horrible sinking feeling in the pit of my stomach that a night of celebration was now turning into an evening of despair. Inspired by their comeback, Portsmouth battered Chelsea for the remaining 20 minutes in pursuit of a winner. They almost got that elusive goal when full-back John McLaughlin's effort hit the crossbar in the dying seconds. But mercifully the Blues hung on and the game ended all square. While it was a bit of a choker to be so close and yet so far, it now set up the home game against dirty Leeds on the following Saturday nicely. How sweet would it be to wave goodbye to the Second Division against one of our bitterest rivals? Three points would mean that we were up.

This Leeds side was a pale shadow of the great team that had dominated in the 1970s, a group that was celebrated and reviled in equal measure for their propensity for dabbling in the dark arts of the game to get a result. Our rivalry with the Yorkshire club had started in the mid-1960s when we seemed to be drawn against them in the FA Cup on a regular basis, culminating in that epic victory over them in the 1970 FA Cup Final. I was confident that we'd get the job done this time in front of what would be a fervent home crowd at the Bridge. The prospect that by Saturday evening Chelsea might once again be a First Division club, after five long years in the wilderness, was tantalising.

I planned to get a lift from our keyboard player, Dave, who was going up to London to buy one of those hideous A-frames for his synths. They had been made popular by the likes of Howard Jones. The plan was that we'd meet up again that evening at the Punch and Judy in Covent Garden for a drink, which for me would be one of celebration, or consolation, dependant upon how the Blues got on.

* * *

On the Friday night before the game, I was having a drink with my mate Tim at the Wagon and Horses in Hemel Hempstead. Tim then went on to tell me what he'd been up to that week. To my amazement, Tim recounted how he'd followed the chef of the Wagon and Horses home one night, to see where he was living, as all of us had a suspicion that he was actually homeless. The reason for the lack of a roof over his head, we thought, was perhaps down to his gross eating habits and lack of personal hygiene, which led to him being christened 'Stig of the Dump', after the kids' TV show and book. Time after time he was thrown out of places where he was sofa surfing, for pulling stunts like bringing home takeaways, eating them in bed and then discarding the remnants of his meals down the side of the bed, where they laid rotting until the stench became unbearable. One of my mates told me that when Stig was finally kicked out of one of the places, they discovered half-eaten kebabs and scraps of detritus that he had thoughtfully left behind. I remember he had a craving for chillis, the hotter the better. In other words, he was, indeed, a human dustbin.

One evening he came out from the kitchen at the pub in his chef whites, which were splattered all down the front with the evidence of what he'd been cooking that week. All of this made the Wagon and Horses the go-to place if you wanted to contract the bubonic plague. Stig was a proud Mancunian, and a rabid United supporter. He used to get misty-eyed when he told us tales about his hometown, and how much nicer it was up north, which left us all wondering why he ever left his beloved Manchester. Tim used to get the bus home from the pub most nights, along with Stig, who would get off first at a stop that was apparently near to where he lived. It seemed that on this particular night, Tim had got off at a request stop further up the hill, and started to follow Stig to see just where he lived. Tim kept what he believed to be a safe distance behind Stig when suddenly he noticed the chef heading back into the direction of the town centre, where they'd both just come from.

As Stig was about to enter into a block of Guinness Trust flats, he suddenly turned round and must have seen Tim in the shadows. At the time Tim was unsure as to whether he'd been spotted; after all, it was late at night, and from that distance he could have been anyone. In an attempt to disguise himself, Tim started walking away with a heavy limp in order to throw Stig off the scent. Tim then carried on walking up the road and disappeared into a side turning where he remained until the coast was clear. Not wishing to push his luck and be caught red-handed by Stig, Tim hid down that side turning until the next bus turned up, and then headed home.

'Did he see you?' was my first question, after I'd finished choking on the beer I'd been drinking while he recounted this bizarre tale.

'I don't think so,' Tim replied. 'I think that limp must have put him off.'

'Bloody hell, Tim. What if he'd seen you?'

'No, no,' said Tim. 'I'm sure I got away with it.'

Twenty minutes later, Stig came into the pub to start his shift in the kitchen. He walked straight past us. It seemed that Tim had indeed got away with it. We both carried on talking until out of nowhere, Stig tapped Tim on the shoulder and said, 'How's the limp, Tim?'

'What do you mean?' Tim replied. By this time, Tim's face was crimson red.

'You know what I'm talking about, you stupid git,' and with that, Stig walked away back to his kitchen, shaking his head.

Tim was lost for words and looked shame-faced, and from that moment on the whole ludicrous incident was never mentioned again. The mystery of where Stig was living remains to this day.

20

SATURDAY, 28 April 1984 was another gloriously sunny spring day. Dave dropped me off at Euston so that he could go off to buy his musical equipment, while I headed for Euston Square, which was my preferred route since I'd first started going to the Bridge in 1968. I took the risk that day of wearing the yellow away shirt which was pushing my luck a bit, as the Leeds mob were known for ambushing lone stragglers whenever they had a day out in London. Sod them, I thought. Today I'm wearing my team's colours, which in retrospect, while being noble and brave, was also extremely reckless.

The atmosphere was electric as Chelsea kicked off and tore straight into Leeds, not giving them a moment's respite on the ball. In fact Leeds looked a right old motley crew. In goal was the 37-year-old David Harvey, who'd played in the 1970 FA Cup Final replay. They also featured the 38-year-old Scottish winger, Peter Lorimer, who had also played in that game 14 years earlier. Lorimer looked decidedly out of shape, carrying quite a bit of timber from consuming what looked like a lot of pies. Don't get me wrong, in his day Lorimer was a fearsome opponent with a tremendous shot, perhaps the hardest striker of a football I've ever seen. Sadly, those days were far behind him as he and his team-mates could do nothing to stem the blue tide that was threatening to engulf them. The dam broke after just six minutes when Micky Thomas hit a fine drive into the top corner of the net at the North End. Straightaway, there was pandemonium followed by a pitch invasion. More was to follow. After some wing wizardry from Pat Nevin, who proceeded to skin three of the Leeds defenders, he then crossed the ball on to the head of Kerry Dixon, who duly despatched his effort past Harvey. Chelsea now sensed blood and just a few minutes later, Kerry got his second with a brilliant chip that completely deceived the hapless Harvey. At half-time it was 3-0 to the Blues. Surely the second half would be nothing more than a formality? But then again, who knows? I always erred on the side of caution, having been bitten by the fickle mistress that was football.

During the break, chairman Ken Bates pleaded through a megaphone for the fans not to invade the pitch again, as the referee had already threatened to call the game off if there was any repeat of this behaviour in the second half. Mr Bates's request seemed to be working when Kerry completed his hat-trick on 52 minutes to put Chelsea 4-0 ahead with a low drive from just outside the box. The crowd, by and large, behaved themselves and stayed put. The remainder of the match was like an exhibition with Chelsea taking their foot off the pedal while Leeds had essentially already thrown the towel in, and seemed extremely keen for the referee to end this horrible nightmare of a day for them.

As the last few minutes approached, crowds were forming in front of the West Stand and in front of Gate 13, for the inevitable pitch invasion, a repeat of the celebrations we'd enjoyed back in the 1976/77 season after a 4-0 thrashing of Hull City when the referee had also threatened to call the game off, which had led to Eddie Mac pleading with the fans to behave. The last thing Chelsea needed now was another goal. The trouble was that no one had informed substitute Paul Canoville. King Canners had other thoughts on his mind as he burst into the box from the right wing and sent a blistering shot past Harvey into the roof of the net from a tight angle. Cue pandemonium as the hordes of Chelsea supporters, so starved of success, once more stormed on to the pitch. For a few minutes, myself and a lot of other people standing next to me at the tea bar were terrified that the referee would indeed abandon the match. Bloody typical, I thought. Only Chelsea could win 5-0, get promoted, and then have the result rubbed out. Thankfully the official saw sense, because as soon as Leeds kicked off he blew the final whistle, which heralded another mass invasion of blue-and-yellow-clad supporters, swarming all over the pitch.

The players were mobbed as the hordes celebrated with as much fervour as I'd ever seen from a crowd at the Bridge. Eventually the squad made their way to the middle tier of the East Stand to take a bow. For all of us there, it was a memory that will live forever. Unbelievably, the police had decided to keep the Leeds supporters in the North End of the ground, to witness one of their most hated rivals celebrate like there was no tomorrow. Why they did this I have no idea. The usual procedure was to keep the home fans in the ground while the away support were shepherded towards Fulham Broadway, to cut down the risk of a clash. The result of the plod's folly was that the Leeds supporters, who were already seething at seeing their team humiliated, started breaking up pieces of the terraces and lobbing the concrete at the police and anyone else unlucky enough to be in their vicinity. In an attempt to calm the situation, Ken Bates, armed with a megaphone, made another plea to the visitors for calm. I don't know if my memory serves me correctly, but I'm convinced that Mr Bates, who was not exactly known for his tact, informed the Leeds supporters through his trusty megaphone, 'Calm down please, lads. Every team has a bad day, and my God, your team has just had a rotten one.'

There then seemed to be a scuffle as the megaphone was pulled out of Batesey's hands, a move that confirmed the police had no more interest in his attempt at keeping the peace. The result of these words was that the Leeds supporters now started aiming their rocks of rubble straight at the electric scoreboard, just behind where they were massed. Under such a barrage the poor old scoreboard didn't stand a chance, and soon it was evident that there was smoke and flames billowing from an electrical fire. Not wanting to stay around now that I'd seen the players receiving their salute from the masses of Blues fans, I made my way out of the ground to head for Covent Garden, where I was due to meet Dave for a night of hitting the beer.

One footnote to that game is that Leeds, who looked a right old rag-tag unit that day, had seemingly forgotten their away socks and had to borrow Chelsea's yellow socks to avoid a clash. It was indicative of just how far Leeds had fallen since the glory days of the early 1970s when manager Don Revie would never have allowed such slipshod practice.

Seeing that I had a bit of time to spare and it was a lovely warm evening, I decided to walk from the Bridge to Covent Garden, which is quite a trek, but what did I care? It gave me a chance to revel in the fact that once more, Chelsea were a top-flight side. I was just around the corner from Covent Garden when I decided to stop off and have a drink at The Cambridge on the corner of Shaftesbury Avenue. For years this had been the preferred watering hole whenever we went to see a film at Leicester Square. As I walked in, I saw some Chelsea boys who were well into their celebrations. Such was the feeling of goodwill that when they saw my yellow away shirt, they asked me what

I was drinking. I didn't need to be asked twice. 'I'll have a pint of Guinness, if that's OK.' 'Coming right up,' was the reply of my brand new brothers in arms.

We spent the next 20 minutes recounting Chelsea's glorious season when I realised that if I didn't get a move on, then I'd be late for meeting Dave at the Punch and Judy. What to do? They had bought me a drink and it would be a bit mean just to say, 'Thanks for that lads, now I'll be on my way.' So I decided to do the decent thing and bought another round which would definitely mean that I'd be late for meeting up with Dave, but who cared? Days like this don't come around very often in the life of a football fan, so I was going to make sure that I enjoyed every second of this brilliant evening.

After finishing my second pint, I said goodbye to the lads and made my way round to Covent Garden to be greeted by Dave, who was standing on the balcony of the Punch and Judy when he asked me, 'Where the hell have you been?'

'Having a drink with some of my Blues brothers. Sorry about that.'

Bloody hell, I thought, he's acting like an angry housewife who's been waiting for hours for her husband to find his way home from the pub. I half expected him to say, 'And you've been drinking!' He then pointed at the main square of Covent Garden and said, 'Take a look at this.' To my amazement there was a sea of blue, white and yellow. It seemed that I wasn't the only Chelsea boy who'd had the same idea.

For the rest of that evening, I got talking to loads of other Blues fans while Dave stood there like a lemon, unable to join in the celebrations due to the fact that he supported Manchester United. Mind you, he did keep to his word that night when he handed over the £20 he owed me for winning the bet that Chelsea would get promoted that season, which had been made in Corfu back in September. On my part, it was a bit of a long shot. Despite Chelsea making a good start to that season, the fact was that we'd almost been relegated during the previous campaign so it was a bit of a punt, but what riled me was when Dave called Chelsea 'Second Division no-hopers'. That comment had made my blood boil. No one was going to get away with that.

But thanks to Chelsea I found myself £20 richer and, more importantly, they found themselves back in the First Division.

* * *

I said earlier that it was very rare to have live football on during the week, so it was a bit of a shock when I found out that the BBC intended to show the first ever live game between two sides in the Second Division. That Friday at 7.15pm the BBC cameras were at Maine Road for the match between Manchester City and Chelsea. This game must have been seen as a potential title showdown, but by this time City's form had floundered, and they were now very much outsiders for promotion. Once again, I watched it at Dave's home. Looking back, he must have been heartily sick of Chelsea by now, and my constant crowing must have been driving him mad.

The first half was goalless as City tried everything to put themselves back in the frame for a last-minute quest for a place in the top tier. After 20 minutes of the second half, it was the yellow-shirted visitors who took the lead when Pat Nevin brilliantly rolled his marker to fire a cross-shot that went in off the post past City keeper Alex Williams. Cue another pitch invasion that thankfully was halted by the scorer himself, who personally pleaded with the excited fans to return to the terraces, which they dutifully did. Five minutes later, Chelsea sealed the victory with a quite brilliant second goal. Paul Canoville shielded the ball from a City defender, and then in an instant sent a reverse pass through his opponent's legs where David Speedie, running on the overlap, centred first time and Kerry Dixon's bullet header flew past Williams into the back of the net. It was a brilliant smash-and-grab goal, and highlighted that Chelsea were indeed a class above any other side in the division. Chelsea easily saw out the last 20 minutes to win 2-0.

Now we could concentrate on taking the title right under the noses of our nearest rivals, Sheffield Wednesday. All we needed was for them to slip up. Our prayers were answered the following day when Wednesday surprisingly lost at Shrewsbury which meant that Chelsea's home game against Barnsley was now taking on titanic proportions. If we could beat them, and if Manchester City could come away with something when they visited Hillsborough to play Wednesday, and I knew that it was a big 'if', then we were in with a decent shout of going up as champions.

That weekend was a bank holiday. I was due to be staying with Clare at her friend's flat, just near Victoria station, which meant that I would be tantalisingly close to the Bridge where Chelsea would be playing Barnsley on the Monday. I'd promised Clare that we'd go out that afternoon with the couple we were staying with. It was in fact a promise I had no intention of keeping. Somehow, don't ask me, but I persuaded the three of them to accompany me to the Bridge, pleading that I just couldn't miss this game. Unbelievably they agreed, and we made our way to the ground. Clare had no interest in football, and her friends, a Greek-Cypriot couple, were decidedly in the same category. Personally, I couldn't stand the sight of them. She was an absolute nightmare who mercilessly bullied the poor sap who happened to be her boyfriend. He was ten years older than the rest of us, and looked like Groucho Marx's long-lost brother. How he put up with her tantrums I'll never know, but as Elvis Costello once said, 'A self-made mug is hard to break.'

With the game locked at 1-1, and Chelsea struggling against a Barnsley team reduced to ten men following a sending off, the stadium announcer took it upon himself to reveal that Sheffield Wednesday were still only drawing with Manchester City at Hillsborough. The effect of this news instantaneously caused the crowd to begin to roar the Blues on and Chelsea surged forward with renewed effort.

In the 77th minute Pat Nevin restored Chelsea's lead, and then fired in his second goal of the game just before full time to give the Blues a vital 3-1 win. My joy fell on deaf ears with the people who'd accompanied me that day, but who cared? Chelsea had the points. And things got even better when it was announced over the PA that Wednesday had only drawn 0-0 with City which meant that if Chelsea, who now led the table, matched the Yorkshire club's result on the final Saturday, they would take the title.

Our last game was away to Grimsby at Blundell Park, while Wednesday were due to play Cardiff at Ninian Park. After Grimsby's 3-2 victory at the Bridge back in December, I was sure that this game would be a tough one. I was also pretty sure that Wednesday wouldn't have it all their own way at Cardiff, a ground where Chelsea had struggled back in March when we came back from 3-0 down to get a 3-3 draw. The wait that week was almost unbearable. Yet again there were moods of positivity that we'd get the result we needed, soon followed by ominous black clouds of doubt. I couldn't get to Grimsby so, once again, I followed tradition, and it was back to my music room to keep up with the latest scores on the radio, which was harrowing.

Soon the news had come through that Wednesday had gone in front at Cardiff, which meant that if the scores stayed the same with Chelsea only drawing, then the Yorkshire club would take the title. In the 38th minute the yellow-shirted Chelsea scored a vital goal when Kerry headed in Nevin's cross. At half-time we were still 1-0 up, but Wednesday were leading as well. I knew that the next 45 minutes would seem an eternity. The feeling of helplessness was almost overwhelming.

I took a break at the interval by walking round the garden. If ever there was a case of a dead man walking then I was most definitely it. Nervously, I made my way back to the music room to face three-quarters of an hour of sheer torture. My heart sank when I heard that Wednesday had gone two up against Cardiff. Why didn't they just get lost, I thought. We deserve the title, not those brawny, muscled thugs from Yorkshire. Though Chelsea could dish it out as well, with the likes of Joey Jones, Micky Thomas and especially David Speedie, Wednesday were the arch exponents of smashing the ball forward at every opportunity, while the Blues played with flair and a quicksilver brand of football that exuded style and elan but also had the ability to mix it with any opponent who wanted a scrap. One thing that I've just remembered is that the Wednesday game kicked off ten minutes before ours at Grimsby because of overcrowding, due to the thousands of Chelsea supporters who had travelled to Blundell Park.

My heart missed a beat when it was announced that Chelsea had been awarded a penalty. The feeling of joy was mixed with fear as our record from the spot that season had been a hit-and-miss affair. Surely a second goal now would finish off Grimsby and their big-mouthed captain,

Joe Waters, who'd announced before the game that he didn't fancy Chelsea for the title. Thankfully his prediction would come to naught, much like his career. My fears were confirmed when Nevin's effort was saved. The agony of the remaining time will live with me forever. Those last few minutes seemed to last for an eternity, but then finally the news came through that Chelsea had won, which confirmed that they were Second Division champions for the first time. Though Wednesday had also won 2-0 at Cardiff, that result was at the end of the day, meaningless.

Unable to contain my joy and relief, I made my way downstairs to watch the scores come in on *Grandstand*. I waited patiently for them to announce that Chelsea were indeed Second Division champions only to be shocked and devastated by the BBC's lack of interest in the Blues' achievements. In fact, the host, I think it could have been Des Lynam, actually announced that Sheffield Wednesday had been promoted, and almost as an afterthought he informed the watching millions with a brief comment of, 'And Chelsea go up as champions.' I felt like sticking one on him. It seemed, indeed, that our achievement in winning that league was deemed as being of very little interest to the Beeb. Newcastle were also promoted that day, finishing third after their 3-1 win against Brighton, and Kevin Keegan announced his retirement from football.

But why should I worry if Chelsea had been given the cold shoulder by the BBC? We had the title, we had the trophy, and after five long years we were back mixing it with the big boys. No more trips to Oldham and Shrewsbury. Now it would be visits to Old Trafford and Anfield. But first I had the summer to look forward to; a summer in which to revel in Chelsea's success. It's hard to believe that the only pieces of merchandise I have from that brilliant season are my blue home shirt, the yellow away shirt, and a Canon League Second Division winners pin badge. This was an era when clubs didn't cash in on their successes. I'm sure that if Chelsea had brought out a special Second Division champions emblem to be worn on the blue shirts for the following season, they would have sold in their thousands. Still, these were the days before football became the cash cow it is now.

After Chelsea won their second Champions League in 2021 against Manchester City in Porto, I went online to the Chelsea Megastore. Within minutes, they had a whole host of Champions League winners merchandise for sale, which shows you how quickly clubs monetise any form of success these days. Supporters of the younger generation, especially those over the last 20 years, will ask what all the fuss is about in winning a Second Division title, especially after two decades of Chelsea becoming serial trophy winners? If you'd lived through those desperate seasons between 1978/79, through to the rebirth of the club in 1983/84, you might have some idea as to why fans of my generation revere that team to this day. The signings made during the summer of 1983 were a masterstoke that transformed the club into a new Chelsea and a new era.

One event huge significance at the club was manager John Neal being taken ill during that game with Grimsby, complaining of chest pains, which turned out to be far more serious than anyone had thought and led to him having heart surgery later than summer. Although he was back in the dugout for the first season back in the First Division, unfortunately he had to step down from his position early in the summer of 1985 due to continuing ill health. The reins were then handed over to Chelsea legend John Hollins. In retrospect it was a job too soon for Ollie, and I'm sure if Neal's health hadn't declined then the club might not have suffered like they did in 1986/87 and the disastrous

1987/88 season. It is my opinion and that of many others of my vintage that Neal is surely one of the greatest managers in our history.

Unlike Mourinho, Conte and Tuchel, Neal didn't have the luxury of a billionaire owner under whom money was no object. That Chelsea side of 1983/84 was built on a shoestring budget. The acquisition of those young players was some of the best business that Chelsea had ever done. The likes of Dixon, Speedie, Nevin and the rest of that exciting side have now gone down in Chelsea folklore. And while their achievements may have been overshadowed by recent triumphs, 1983/84 – alongside the FA Cup win of 1969/70 and not forgetting promotion in 1976/77 – is one of my three standout seasons of supporting the Blues. That unlikely triumph of 1983/84 was a shining beacon of hope that pierced the darkness and gloom of the previous five years, and I for one, am honoured to say I was there.

EPILOGUE

ON SATURDAY, 25 August 1984, I left home early to head to Chelsea's first game back in the First Division, at Arsenal. I can even remember what I wore that day: a royal blue Lyle and Scott V-neck sweater with my yellow Chelsea shirt underneath, Lois jeans, and Gola trainers. Just before I arrived at Highbury on that beautiful morning, I helped an elderly lady across the road, hoping that this act of kindness would be rewarded with the Blues getting a result.

The first glimpse I got of new signing Doug Rougvie and the Chelsea players warming up was when I walked up the steps to take my place on the Clock End terrace. That day has gone down in club history as being one of the best away days the Blues have ever enjoyed. There were 20,000 Chelsea fans packed into the Clock End, and I was in the middle of the explosion of joy when Kerry Dixon's brilliant volley equalised after Arsenal had taken the lead four minutes earlier. Chelsea showed no sign of being intimidated and were more than a match for Arsenal. All ended well as the game finished in a 1-1 draw.

One abiding memory I have of the second half was the stick dished out to Arsenal forward Tony Woodcock by the massed ranks of Chelsea supporters. Woodcock had received a driving ban the previous week, and every time he stood in our goalmouth when the Gooners had a corner he got serenaded with, 'Tony's got a bus pass.' I have to say that he took it very well, giving us the thumbs up on more than one occasion. I can recall standing on that terrace like it was yesterday, and alongside the Chelsea supporters on the Stretford End back in 1970, it's one of the best two away days that I've ever experienced.

The Blues went on to have a fine season back in the top flight. One of the highlights for me was the 6-2 thumping of Coventry, who'd taken an early 2-0 lead before Chelsea woke up and put the Midlanders to the sword. Another game that stands out is the 3-1 home win over Liverpool with David Speedie, in particular, sending the Merseysiders home with their tails between their legs. What made it even more impressive was that Liverpool were, at the time, the holders of the First Division title, the European Cup and the League Cup. That result would have been beyond our wildest dreams only a few seasons before. Having said that, Liverpool always seemed to struggle at the Bridge. That afternoon in the autumn of 1984 will always be the one that stands out for me, as two-goal Speedo delivered one of the best performances I'd ever seen from him in the famous royal blue shirt. He gave the Liverpool centre-back pairing of Mark Lawrenson and Alan Hansen one of the biggest runarounds they'd suffered in their careers.

There was also the epic 4-3 victory over Everton at Goodison Park, against the team that would go on to win the league that year. Just before Christmas, Chelsea had signed ex-Fulham striker Gordon Davis. Though it was a brief affair, he grabbed a memorable hat-trick at Goodison. The victory over Sheffield Wednesday in the quarter-final of the League Cup is a bittersweet memory for me. The fact that we triumphed after three memorable games is tarnished by the fact that we lost to Sunderland in the semi-finals when everything that could go wrong did go horribly wrong. That final was contested by Norwich and Sunderland, who were both relegated that year, meaning our failure to win our first major trophy in years is something that still sticks in my craw. Having said that, the period from 1983 to 1985 was like a phoenix rising from the ashes. After years in the wilderness, that team managed by John Neal led everyone who had blue blood in their veins into bright sunlit uplands once more.